HAMLYN GUIDE TO
SKIING

HAMLYN GUIDE TO
SKIING

MARTIN HECKELMAN

HAMLYN

To the international skiing community, to all my family and friends, to Steve and Susie and to the memory of my mother who always encouraged me to follow my dreams

Photographic acknowledgements
Front and back jacket, front and back endpapers, and all photographs other than those listed below were taken in Val d'Isère, France, by Jean-Christophe Souillac using a Nikon FA 35mm camera with an 3.5 FPS (frame per second) motordrive and Fuji 50 RPF transparency film.

Title page: Steve Falconer; photos 33 a,c,e: Martin Heckelman; photos 33b, 40b, 60 and 95 a–e: Kim Lindquist; photo 96a: Daniel Rose at Les Arcs, France; photos 96 b–e: Daniel Rose at Val d'Isère.

First published 1986 by
The Hamlyn Publishing Group Ltd,
Bridge House, London Road,
Twickenham, Middlesex

ISBN 0 600 50121 3

Edited by Derek Hall/Format Publishing Services
Designed by Tony Truscott

Printed and bound by Graficromo s.a., Spain

Contents

Foreword

Skiing has become an immensely popular sport worldwide, and understandably so. It is exciting, invigorating and healthy, it is undertaken for the most part in beautiful natural conditions, and it has the merit of being a sporting activity which an entire family of widely differing ages can enjoy as a holiday together.

My family was lucky enough to encounter Martin Heckelman at an important time in our skiing. My wife was giving serious thought to abandoning it after a discouraging accident, and the children were either putting on skis for the first time or working laboriously through the beginner's instructions.

I welcome the opportunity of writing this foreword to thank Martin for the many subsequent accident-free holidays we have enjoyed and for making us a family of accomplished skiers. I hope also to encourage others to read his book and follow his methods so that they, too, may have the pleasure of skiing with confidence, safety and delight in all conditions.

Martin's secret has been to analyse the fundamentals that go into the basic parallel ski turn and then to evolve a course of instruction which imparts to the pupil these essentials so naturally that he or she absorbs them almost imperceptibly and thus emerges remarkably quickly as an accomplished skier. At times I must admit that I have found some of the contributing exercises seemingly misplaced, if not comical. 'What could be the point of doing this?', I have asked myself—only to find a fault subsequently cured or unexpected progress made. It is subsequent realization of the link between the two that has alerted me to Martin's special achievement: working out that link, analysing why it should operate and understanding how it can be imparted to the pupil.

The correct basic position, control and style follow in painless sequence in the teaching system that Martin calls the 'International Parallel Technique' for beginners, and the 'Tea-for-two Ski Dance' for all others (you see what I mean by comic and seemingly pointless exercises?), but from them come quickly and naturally the effortless and stylish skill which marks the accomplished skier.

If you wish to acquire this expertise and confidence, to enjoy the instruction on the way and to penetrate the simple mysteries of this thrilling sport, I can only recommend that you read on!

Robin Leigh-Pemberton
Governor of the Bank of England

Acknowledgements

To thank all the people who have helped me during my career as a ski instructor in the USA, Europe and South America would require too much space. Every ski instructor, ski school director, and student with whom I have had the pleasure of working has taught me something. I, therefore, would like to extend my gratitude collectively to all these friends. I must, nonetheless, mention a few people to whom I am most indebted:

Walter Foeger, for having developed the 'Natur-Teknik' system of ski instruction which emphasized natural body movements and eliminated the need for teaching snowplough and stem turns to novice skiers. Walter's general philosophies of ski instruction have been included in the International Parallel Technique (TIP).

Adrian Duvillard, the French ski champion, and Eva Duvillard, who were instrumental in helping me obtain my first ski instructor position in France in the highly rated Megève Ski School, and for Adrian's expert technical advice while I was learning to adapt to the modern French system of skiing.

Jean-Claude Killy, who convinced me of the value of independent leg action with the skis not locked together which proved invaluable for skiing the steep slopes and gullies.

Henri Duvillard, the former downhill, slalom and giant slalom champion, for allowing me to train with him on his home slopes, and for the many pointers that he gave me on the most advanced slalom and giant slalom techniques, which I was then able to incorporate into my skiing and eventually, as it evolved, into the International Parallel Technique.

Daniel Rose, Steve Falconer, Kim Lindquist, Jean-Denis LaGarde and Ian Foster for their excellence as ski photographers. Their combined efforts enabled me to have a complete set of high-quality photographs to show to publishers, along with my manuscript. Though only a few of these photographs appear, had the ski equipment used been the latest, the complete set would certainly have graced the book.

Jean-Christophe Souillac, a superb skier, ski instructor and photographer whose talents, patience, energy, endurance, ideas and perfectionism resulted in the vast majority of the splendid photographs that accompany the text.

My sister and brother-in-law, Myrna and Murray Drillich, as well as John and Priscilla Sadler, Derek and Claire Merfield and Daniel Rose for their kindness, generosity and valuable suggestions while I was writing this book.

Robin and Rose Leigh-Pemberton for their encouragement, and for Robin's kind testimony which contributed to convincing publishers of the book's merit.

Kim Lindquist, Anthony Bourke and Henry Schniewind for having performed the aerial jumping manoeuvres.

Ian and Jan Carling, Dan and Carol Behrman, Cindy, Jan and Craig Drillich, Lindsey Irwin, Barney and Sylviane Radoff, Patricia Killy, David McCallum, Susie Fischer, Laverne Waddington, Anthony Goldstein and Peter Sprague for their myriad contributions.

Fischer Skis, Dynafit Ski Boots, Tyrolia Bindings, Event Skiwear, Fuji Film France, Pouilloux-Vaurnet Glasses, La Poudreuse, Top Ski, Jean Sport and Killy ski shops, Dann Photo, La Coupe and the Maison de la Presse of Val d'Isère, for providing excellent equipment and service.

A final special acknowledgement is due to the ski area of Val d'Isère, France, where all the action photographs were taken.

Martin Heckelman

Introduction

Skiing is one of the easiest sports to learn when taught correctly. Unlike tennis or golf, it is not necessary to spend years or even months practising and training to become reasonably proficient, and most ski schools can have complete novices confidently stem turning down easy slopes within seven days.

This book aims to achieve far more than that. By following the exercises in Section One, complete novices should, within five days, be able to make controlled parallel turns of the type made by advanced skiers. Furthermore, at the end of these five days they will have developed the correct basic skills to enable them to progress quickly to the many advanced skiing manoeuvres described in Sections Two and Three. By practising the various exercises presented in Sections Two and Three, intermediate and experienced skiers can learn how to perform all the advanced skiing manoeuvres which will permit them to ski confidently and safely on easy and difficult terrain, on moguls, in powder snow, on ice and in all types of 'off-piste' (off-trail) snow conditions.

The International Parallel Technique (TIP), which is introduced in Section One for beginners, is a method of instruction that is simple, safe and successful. It has evolved over many years, and combines what I have found to be the best teaching features of a large number of skiing systems from around the world. The TIP method is not, therefore, a radical new skiing technique. Although the approach is different, the classic parallel turn that one learns is the same as that taught in most modern ski schools in Europe and America. The major difference between a novice learning by the TIP method and other methods lies in the amount of control, precision and confidence the student exhibits after only five days on skis, and in the rapidity of development of advanced skiing skills.

Instead of teaching novices to ski by the traditional snowplough and stem turn approach, the TIP method breaks down the basic parallel turn into individual body movements. Ski exercises are designed to teach the body how to perform these movements, and then integrate them to produce a smooth, parallel, carved turn.

Because almost all of these exercises have been drawn from the teaching curricula of the many national skiing systems, skiers who have already learnt to ski, or plan to learn to ski in any organized ski school–whatever the country–should find the photographs and descriptions of these exercises very useful as a supplement to their ski school lessons. In fact, regardless of which country they are in, they should find among the exercises many of the ski manoeuvres that they are being taught. For the benefit of those of you who intend to use this book to help you improve and further your skiing abilities, the book has been organized as a self-teaching manual for step-by-step development from beginner to advanced skier.

Section One contains the nine steps of the TIP method and is intended for beginners and for those intermediate skiers who would benefit from revision of their basic skiing skills. These nine interlocking steps are described separately, and it is best to practise each step in the order shown. At the end of five days and the ninth step, even complete novices should be making smooth and linked parallel turns on easy intermediate slopes and can then proceed to the more advanced techniques described in the subsequent sections.

Intermediate skiers wishing to proceed to advanced levels should go through the basic steps, but at an accelerated pace, commencing with the traverse, and concluding with the parallel downhill turn, with particular emphasis on skating. This latter step is unfortunately often neglected in many current teaching techniques for adults. I especially recommend that intermediate skiers, and indeed many of you who consider yourselves to be advanced skiers, practise the staircase sidesliding exercises at slow speeds in order to improve the sensitivity of your edge control.

Section Two is intended for intermediate skiers who are ready to become advanced skiers, and for experienced skiers wishing to improve their ski technique and skills in the more difficult manoeuvres. This section teaches the advanced skiing position, and explains all advanced ski techniques and manoeuvres, including avalement and the jet turn. In addition, it describes safe techniques for skiing steep gullies and mountain faces, and how to ski on ice and wind-blown crust.

Section Three is devoted to techniques of skiing in powder and 'off-piste' snow. It shows the intermediate/advanced skier how to adjust his or her basic technique to ski powder and 'off-piste' snow confidently, demonstrating and explaining 11 different methods of coping with the varied snow conditions.

Naturally, learning from a book is not as easy as having a competent instructor in front of you demonstrating the manoeuvres and correcting any errors you may be making on the spot. I have therefore tried to make the explanations of the various steps involved clear and precise, and have made extensive use of detailed stop-action photographs to complement the text. Furthermore, I have attempted, through the numerous additional tips and notes, to supplement the basic explanations in order to help you understand the 'key' or 'secrets' of each ski manoeuvre.

I hope that everybody who reads this book will find the details on ski techniques valuable, and that by practising and incorporating these you will be able to ski more safely and more easily, and will gain greater enjoyment of one of the world's finest sporting activities. My ultimate aim is that you should continue to use this book to help develop the skills that will allow you to ski every type of terrain, in every possible snow condition, in complete confidence.

Alpine skiing

Skiing is one of the fastest growing participation sports in the world, and this is perfectly understandable since it is a very healthy, fun-filled way to enjoy winter.

There are two primary types of skiing—Alpine and Nordic—and they require very different equipment and locales. Most Nordic skiing, which is also referred to as 'cross-country skiing', is performed basically on flat or gently rolling terrain. The skis used are quite narrow and very light, the shoes are normally made of leather and are similar to running shoes and the bindings allow the heels of the Nordic ski shoes to lift, enabling the skier to glide, walk or run on his or her skis.

Alpine skiing—the most popular form of skiing and the style described in this book—is, for the most part, performed on snow-covered hills and mountains that vary in gradient from very gentle inclines to extremely steep mountain faces. A novice skier naturally starts on the gentle terrain, and progresses to the more demanding terrain after developing the necessary technique and capability to control his or her skis on the steeper slopes and at higher speeds.

The skis used for Alpine skiing have slippery plastic soles and sharp metal edges that are used for controlling and steering the skis. The ski boots are normally made of plastic and are heavier and more voluminous than ordinary street shoes. These boots are designed to fit comfortably on the foot and at the same time hold the foot and ankle firmly in place so that they do not feel any strain during the skiing movements. The boots allow the ankle to bend forward but not sideways. The bindings which secure the skis to the boots contain springs designed to release the boot and skier during a fall.

A form of skiing combining Alpine and Nordic skiing is growing in popularity in many parts of the world, especially the western USA, Australia and New Zealand. It is known as 'three-pin skiing', 'skinny-skis skiing', 'Norpine' or 'Tele-mark', and uses a lightweight ski similar to, though slightly wider than, a Nordic ski, and with metal edges. The binding is called a 'three-pin' and lifts at the heel. The boots used are made of leather and are similar to hiking shoes.

Other forms of Alpine skiing that are becoming very popular are 'monoskiing' and 'surf skiing'. Both are performed on the same slopes as normal Alpine skiing. Monoskiing is very similar to standard skiing, except that one stands on a very wide board with both feet attached to the board using standard Alpine bindings. The ski boots are the same as for Alpine skiing. While monoskiing can be performed on moguls and packed slopes it is most fun in deep powder snow or in wind-blown or heavy snow.

Surf skiing is also executed on a wide board but one uses firm 'après-ski' boots and stands on the board sideways, hooking the boots through straps attached to the board. The stance and the technique for turning are quite similar to water surfing.

Choosing your equipment

While most modern ski equipment can be quite expensive, especially at the top end of the range, beginners do not need to purchase the most expensive equipment. Each ski manufacturer has skis designed especially for beginners, intermediates and advanced skiers, with the beginners' skis being the least expensive. Similarly, boot manufacturers offer models for all standards of skiers, with prices corresponding with the standard of the boot.

In fact, rather than purchasing, it is advisable for beginners to hire their equipment from a reliable ski shop or hire company. By hiring, you have the opportunity of trying a variety of products before deciding what is best for you. Furthermore, a beginner will probably prefer relatively short skis to start with and then progress to longer skis as improvement is made. Consequently, by hiring, you can easily upgrade your equipment to correspond to your current level and type of skiing. Most ski centres have excellent rental shops with a wide variety of the latest equipment from which to choose.

Whether you plan to buy or rent your ski equipment you should always deal with a reputable ski shop which employs knowledgeable staff. It is worth chatting with the salesperson and allowing him or her to help you choose the right gear.

Skis

There are various charts which correlate weight, height, skiing ability and the type of skiing you prefer with the length of ski to use. Basically, shorter skis are recommended for beginners, as they are lighter and easier to manoeuvre. Longer skis are recommended for more accomplished skiers because they perform better at higher speeds.

A simple approach is to choose a pair of skis that reach 15 cm (6 in) below your head if you are a complete beginner; approximately head

height or 10 cm (4 in) above your head if you have skied a few times; approximately 15–25 cm (6–10 in) above your head if you are an intermediate skier; and an arm's length above your head if you are an advanced skier wanting to ski fast. The chart below provides a more accurate means of determining your proper ski length.

Ski length calculator

Enter points for your weight		A
Over 91 kg (Over 200 lb)		155
73–90 kg (160–199 lb)		150
55–72 kg (120–159 lb)		145
36–54 kg (80–119 lb)		140
Under 35 kg (Under 80 lb)		135

Enter points for your ability		B
(see below for definitions of target groups)		
Target Group S		45
Target Group A		30
Target Group L		25

Enter points for your height		C
Over 1.8 m (Over 5 ft 11 in)		15
1.6–1.79 m (5 ft 3 in–5 ft 10 in)		10
Under 1.59 m (Under 5 ft 2 in)		5

Total A + B + C ⬚ is your ideal ski length (in centimetres)

Your target group

Using the definitions below you can easily assign yourself to one of three target groups. This will help you find skis which are matched to your ability and make the ski length calculation above. **Target group L:** beginners or those who can ski parallel on easy slopes only and at slow speeds. **Target group A:** intermediates who can ski parallel on moderate gradients and easy snow conditions at medium speeds. **Target group S:** experts who can ski all types of slope, snow and gradient at higher speeds.

The brand of ski that you choose can be based on appearance or cost; provided you buy a ski from a well-known manufacturer, it will conform to the specifications laid down. A ski for a beginner will be cheaper than a ski for an advanced-level skier, and is designed to be used at relatively slow speeds on easy slopes. Because it is meant to turn easily at slow speeds it will be much easier for a beginner to handle this ski rather than trying to learn on an advanced-level ski. A good ski shop should have literature from the ski manufacturer describing the intended uses for the different models.

Ski boots

This is probably the most important piece of ski equipment that you will use, and therefore you should take the most care in choosing it. The reason for this is that skiing, or learning to ski, with aching, uncomfortable feet is very tiring and painful.

To ski properly and remain in control you will have to press your shins forward against the tongue of the boot. If this tongue is hard or unyielding it very quickly causes the shins to become tender and sore, making it painful to press forward, which will in turn make it difficult to control your skis. If the boots do not support you laterally, you can easily develop ankle pains. If the boots fit too tightly, in addition to discomfort and/or foot cramping you may experience a decrease in the blood circulation to your feet causing them to become very cold. So take your time selecting a pair of boots that is right for you.

Most of the ski shops in ski centres carry one or two brands of rental boots. It is a good idea to try on several pairs of boots until you find a pair that feel perfectly comfortable. If none of the boots in your selected ski shop feels right, try some different brands of boots in other ski shops until you find some that fit properly.

In the early days of modern skiing the boots were made of leather. If a pair of boots fitted well in the shop they would probably be unsatisfactory on the slopes since they would usually stretch with use, and would no longer give the firm support required. Consequently, the rule of thumb was that a pair of boots needed to feel too tight when worn in the shop in order to have a proper fit. With the advent of plastic boots, this philosophy no longer applies; a boot that feels comfortable in the shop will probably feel comfortable on the slopes. A boot that hurts your foot in the shop will definitely hurt your foot on the slopes. The advantage of renting boots is that you can exchange them if they don't feel comfortable and can keep exchanging them until you find a pair that is right for you.

When you find the right boot you may decide to purchase a pair of the same model. If the new boot has an anatomic flow inner system (a soft foam that takes the form of your foot and ankle) you may have to wear them for some hours until the flow adjusts to your foot. In this case it is best to have the boots buckled loosely at first, and to then tighten them as the inner boots mould themselves to your feet.

Some boots have a bladder that can be pumped up with compressed air, providing a comfortable cushion around the foot. Most of these systems are found in beginner and intermediate boots.

The system which provides the most comfort and control is a foam-injected inner boot that moulds to the shape of your foot. Some boot manufacturers offer foam injection in their higher performance models. To have foam injection incorporated in other model boots, you can purchase a separate inner boot that can be foam injected in any make of outer shell to ensure a very comfortable, snug fit. Orthotics or inner soles that mould to the shape of the bottom of your foot and can then be inserted into the boots are very welcome additions. Resting your feet on footbeds specially designed for them provides for great comfort and aids in controlling ski edging.

Boots for beginners tend to be softer and easier to flex forward than advanced-level boots, which are designed to handle the stresses of high-speed turns. Beginners who wear advanced-model ski boots will probably find it more difficult to control their skis than if they used boots designed for beginners.

In recent years, rear entry boots have gained in popularity, and most manufacturers now produce a boot of this type, particularly for beginners and intermediate skiers. While there are some rear entry boots for advanced skiers on the market, most racing boots and top of the range models are front entry, and are secured with either four or five buckles. Having skied with both front and rear entry boots, I have chosen to use front entry because of the precise control that I get from the buckle arrangement. However, depending on the shape of your foot, the width, the instep, the arch and the shape of your ankle, you may find one format better suited to you than the other. What is important is that your heel and ankle are held firmly in place, although the heel may lift approximately 6 mm ($\frac{1}{4}$ in). There should be enough room for your toes to wiggle when you are pressing your shins forward and there should be a snug fit around your instep without causing undue pressure. Therefore the best way to establish which boot is right for you is to try as many different models as possible, both in the shops and on the slopes.

Ski bindings

While ski boots are the most important equipment for comfort, ski bindings are the most important for safety. Regardless of your skiing ability you must have a safe, reliable binding that will open and release you from your skis during awkward falls. Beginners and experts alike should therefore buy the top of the range of any of the known, recognized brands of bindings.

Each manufacturer makes a number of very good bindings designed for different skiers. Racers and heavy, fast skiers need a binding with a very strong spring, while lighter skiers (including children) and beginners require a spring that will release with less stress. A good ski shop can help you choose the binding that is designed for you and, using DIN calculations, can help you determine the proper spring setting for it.

Ski poles

Ski poles are quite inexpensive. A good pole should be light and strong, and should have a comfortable hand grip with some form of safety strap or grip format that allows your hand to release easily from the pole in a fall or if the pole gets snagged. An easy way to determine the proper length for your ski poles is to invert the pole, rest the end of the handle on the floor, flex (bend) your knees and grasp the pole just under the basket. The length is correct when your forearm is parallel to the ground.

Ski clothing

It is much more comfortable, and much warmer, to wear a number of thin layers than to wear one or two very heavy, bulky garments. Closest to the skin it is best to wear a pair of thin long johns or upper and lower separates made of polypropylene or chlorofiber (which transfers the body moisture away to the outer garments). On top of this wear a cotton T-shirt, a polo neck or, as the Americans call it, a turtleneck shirt, and a woollen sweater. For the outer garment, a down, 'Thinsulate' or fibre-filled jacket or parka should keep out most chills. On especially cold days, you may want to add an additional layer, such as a cotton or woollen shirt under the sweater. On warm days you can, of course, remove as many layers as you wish. Garments made from 'Gore-Tex' seem to be one of the best choices for the outer layers. A useful feature of modern ski clothing is that it can be fashionably worn at home as well as on the slopes, so that you are not limiting your investment in top-quality clothing just to skiing holidays.

Trousers

Because beginners tend to fall often, it is a good idea to wear a pair of trousers made from nylon or Gore-Tex over jeans or cotton trousers. This will prevent the undergarments from getting wet. Better still, wear a salopette (bib 'n' brace) or overall which has a water-resistant outer layer, or a one-piece insulated snow suit.

Socks

The rule of thumb used to be to wear two pairs of socks; usually a thin silk or cotton pair under a thicker woollen pair. Most of the modern ski boots now contain insulating materials for warmth, and for the best fit it is now generally recommended that you wear one pair of medium thick cotton, silk or woollen socks only. My experience is that except on the very coldest days one pair of ski socks is sufficient to keep your feet comfortable. On extremely cold days you can

A properly equipped skier should have good-quality skis, top-grade bindings, firm and comfortable ski boots, warm and waterproof outer garments, Gore-Tex or leather insulated gloves and high-quality sunglasses.

keep your feet warm by placing your ski boots in insulating boot covers.

Gloves

A good pair of leather or Gore-Tex insulated gloves or mittens is essential to keep your hands warm. A pair of mittens with woollen liners also works well. On very cold days, if your gloves or mittens are not warm enough, you can wear a thin silk glove closest to the skin to add a layer of warmth. I have found down or 'Thinsulate' filled leather mittens to be the warmest.

Hats

A warm hat that can also cover your ears is very important when trying to keep warm, since a great deal of body heat is lost via an uncovered head.

Sunglasses and goggles

Sunglasses are extremely important. The sun's rays are very strong at high altitudes and their effect is multiplied by the reflections from the snow, and this can cause serious problems to unprotected eyes. It is therefore worth investing in good-quality sunglasses that filter out the sun's damaging ultra-violet rays. These same sunglasses will be very useful for boating, or beach activities in the summer months. Every skier should own a good pair of fog-free goggles for those days when the sun is hiding behind the clouds, making the terrain difficult to see (a condition known as 'flat light') and during snow storms. The best goggles to use have two bonded lenses which are designed to prevent the goggles from fogging.

Accessories

Weather in the mountains can change very rapidly, and a skier should always be prepared for these sudden climatic changes. A knapsack or bag worn on a belt around the waist is very useful for carrying the extra gear to cope with changes in the weather. It is useful to carry a nylon windcheater (windbreaker) which, when folded, takes up very little space, but when worn either under or over your jacket adds considerable warmth. A face mask made of neoprene, silk, leather or wool can be very useful when caught in a blizzard. A cotton or silk scarf worn around the neck is also useful in preventing loss of body heat. A pair of mittens or an inner glove liner can be added when the weather becomes particularly cold. A good pair of fog-free goggles should also be stowed in the bag, as well as a warm hat and an extra pair of dry ski socks. A bar of chocolate, or a bag of nuts and raisins, is a good reserve to have available when needed. It is also worth carrying a bar of paraffin or ski wax that can be rubbed on the bottom of your skis if the snow conditions cause them to stick to the snow, and a screwdriver, Swiss army knife, or binding adjustment key for coping with binding problems.

Because the snow reflects the heat and rays of the sun, it can often get very warm during the afternoons when the sun rises overhead, and so a ski sack is a handy place to stow unneeded layers of clothing.

Finally, suntan cream with a high sunscreen factor should be applied daily to your face, ears and lips for protection from the sun and wind. In the springtime it is a good idea to apply the cream several times a day.

Getting into shape

Skiing can be exhausting, because you use muscles that you don't often use in daily living. Consequently a beginner, or even an experienced skier starting a new season, may ache or feel tired after a few ski sessions. It is advisable, therefore, to get yourself into good physical condition before heading out to the ski slopes. Each person may prefer his or her own approach to fitness, but it is necessary to work on both aerobic and physical conditioning.

Some good aerobic activities include jogging, running, fast walking, bicycling, competitive rowing, speed skating, swimming, cross-country skiing, skipping with a rope, modern dance routines and participation in a daily aerobic exercise programme.

Physical conditioning can be done in your home or at a gymnasium and should consist of a programme of muscle stretching, and exercises designed to increase your strength. Important areas to concentrate on are your thigh, calf, stomach and lower back muscles. Dead weights, springs, proprietary exercise equipment, or simple exercises such as sit-ups and leg lifts can be used to build up and, more importantly, tone up your body's muscles. The better shape you are in when you start to ski the easier you will find it and the quicker will be your progress.

The International Parallel Technique (TIP)

The goal of the International Parallel Technique (TIP), which is described in this section, is for you to be making smooth, linked, parallel turns on an easy intermediate slope at the end of five days.

To reach this level of accomplishment, a series of interlocking steps are presented in an organized order, starting with simple manouevres and going on to more complex manouevres. Each step is designed to build upon the fundamentals that you will have learnt in the previous steps, in the same way as a building is constructed–layer by layer upon the previous layers.

The Beginner Exercises that are performed on Day 1 are designed to teach you to feel more comfortable on your skis, as well as control your skis while you are moving, and set a solid foundation for the subsequent steps. The Traverse position, which is the second step, is the position that the skier is in almost all the time, and the exercises that are presented are designed to teach the body how to assume this position comfortably. Most of the exercises of the TIP are actual ski manoeuvres used in advance skiing and thus, while you are practising these exercises in order to develop basic skills, you are at the same time perfecting advanced skiing capabilities.

The nine interlocking steps which make up the TIP are as follows:

Day 1–Morning: beginner exercises
Day 1–Afternoon: traverse
Day 2–Morning: sidesliding
Day 2–Afternoon: skating and learning to ride ski-lifts
Day 3–Morning: uphill turns
Day 3–Afternoon: pressure turns
Day 4–Morning and afternoon: parallel turns downhill
Day 5–Morning: linked parallel turns on gentle slopes
Day 5–Afternoon: linked parallel turns on intermediate slopes

Experience from teaching novices has convinced me that those who practise the most exercises make the greatest progress afterwards, so I recommend that you take the time to practise and perfect as many of the exercises presented as possible in the order shown.

Beginner exercises

(Day 1 Morning)

The purpose of these exercises is:

- To learn to feel the skis as an extension of your body.
- To learn to develop a sense of balance on the skis while gliding and schussing.
- To learn to shift your weight from ski to ski.
- To learn to change direction while standing still.
- To learn to climb a hill.
- To learn to get up after a fall.
- To learn to do a kick turn.
- To learn to stop at slow speeds on gentle terrain.

When learning any new sport there is an initial period of difficulty as your body adapts to the new demands placed upon it. In skiing, first boots are attached to your feet, then skis are attached to your boots, and suddenly you have a metre or so extension in front of your toes and behind your heel. When you try to turn in the normal manner you find that you step on your skis. Your boots seem heavy and the skis clumsy, and when you stand on a slight gradient, your skis want to slide away from you. All beginners go through this frustrating period so there is no need for undue concern. The Beginner Exercises teach your body to adjust to the fact that your feet have now 'grown' fore and aft, and that they now have slippery plastic bottoms and sharp metal edges.

At the end of the first morning you will realize that the plastic bottoms allow the skis to slide, and that the metal edges digging into the snow enable the skis to turn or stop. You will also feel more comfortable on the skis and will be ready to learn more advanced manoeuvres.

The exercises which follow are those of the International Parallel Technique used for teaching beginners. I recommend that you read through this section carefully.

These exercises are to be performed on flat terrain

1 The basic position on skis

As you can see in pictures 2a and 2b, the body should be facing down the hill and comfortably balanced over both skis, the knees slightly bent, the skis a little less than hip distance apart, the shins leaning against the fronts of the boots, the back in a normal relaxed position, the head centred, the shoulders relaxed and the arms held in front of the body with the elbows bent as though a tray were being carried, and the ski poles pointing slightly backwards.

Special tip

- The ski poles should be worn around the wrist so that you grasp the strap and the grip simultaneously. An easy way to learn to do this is to hold one pole in front of you and let the strap dangle. Place your hand up from the bottom through the strap, as in the picture below left, and then grasp the strap and the grip. As you can see in the picture below right, there is a left and right ski pole. The straps overlap to the left or right so as to be smooth in your hand when you hold the grip.

 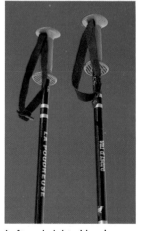

Ski poles worn on the wrist.   Left and right ski poles.

2a

2a and 2b: Basic position on skis.

2b

2 Walking and gliding on skis – with and without ski poles

Keeping the body in the basic position, begin to 'walk' forward by pushing one foot in front of the other. This is accomplished by shuffling one ski forward and then shuffling the other ski forward, shifting your weight alternately from the front foot to the back foot. It is best to try this with the aid of the ski poles for a few strides and then, as in pictures 3a and 3b, by holding the ski poles in the middle and gliding forward without their aid.

4a

3a

4b

4a–d: Turning in position with ski tails as pivot.

3 Turning in position using tails and shovels as pivots

Now that you have taken a few paces forward, it is time to turn around to walk back. This is easily accomplished by taking little steps in a circle, using either the tails (backs of the skis) or shovels (fronts of the skis) to pivot about. Let's start with the tail pivot and turn to the right (clockwise), as shown in picture sequence 4.

Keeping your body in the basic position, lean on the left foot so as to reduce the weight on the right foot and, leaving both ski tails in the same place, step the front of the right ski to the right. Now lean on this ski and lift the front of the left ski and bring it alongside the right ski, leaving the

3b

3a and 3b: Gliding on flat terrain without the aid of ski poles.

4c

4d

The same exercise should be carried out using the shovels of the skis as a pivot. In performing this manoeuvre, the shovel of the ski is kept in place and the tails of the skis are walked around to the right (anticlockwise) completing a circle (picture sequence 5); then to the left (clockwise), completing a circle.

5a

5b

tails in the same place. Repeat this motion of stepping the front of the right ski to the side, followed by the front of the left ski, leaving the tails of both skis in place. This will result in a 'fan' shape and if you continue around you will outline a circle in the snow (picture 4d). This procedure should then be repeated to the left (anticlockwise), again using the tails as a pivot.

Special tip

● If you find that you are placing one ski on the other it is because you are not leaving the tails in place in the snow.

5a–c: Turning in position with ski shovels as pivot.   5c

6a

6a and 6b: Straight schussing down fall-line.   6b

These exercises are to be performed on a gentle slope with an uphill runout

4 Straight schussing down the fall-line

First, it is necessary to understand the term 'fall-line'. This is the steepest path down the section you are on, and thus the direction in which you would slide if you fell, or the path down which a snowball would roll. The significance of the fall-line is that when your skis are pointing down it, they will automatically slide; only when your skis are perpendicular or at right angles to the fall-line will you be able to stand still without relying on your ski poles. This exercise is the first time that you will experience the feeling of skiing, in other words, the skis sliding over the snow–hopefully with you standing on them!

Assume the basic position again, pointing down the fall-line, with your ski poles in the snow preventing you from sliding forwards. So that you do not fall backwards, it is very important to lean against the front of the ski boots as the skis slide and not to lean backwards. Maintain the weight on both feet, relax, release the ski poles with a little push (pictures 6a and 6b), and try to keep your balance as you glide down the hill. If you are on a hill with an uphill runout, as suggested, you will stop automatically as you lose momentum on the uphill slope.

At this point, having successfully made it down the hill, most of my students break out into their first big happy smile, and the ones that get a particular gleam in their eyes are the ones that I know are hooked on skiing for life.

5 Sidestepping up the hill

Having made it down, it would be fun to do it again. To get back up, we sidestep. This is a simple manoeuvre, achieved by keeping the skis perpendicular to the fall-line and walking the skis up the hill using the metal edges to bite into the snow to prevent the skis slipping sideways.

7e

7c

7d

7b

7a

Assuming the basic position, you should stand with your skis perpendicular to the fall-line as shown in picture 7a. It is absolutely essential to incline your knees and ankles towards the uphill slope the entire time in order to bite the edge into the snow. Lean on the lower ski and move the upper ski up the hill in a small step, as shown in picture 7b. Place the ski in the snow perpendicular to the fall-line and place your weight on this ski, pressing so that the edge bites into the snow, as in picture 7c. Now lift the lower ski (picture 7d) and place it alongside the upper ski and again lean on this lower ski, being sure to incline your knee and ankle towards the uphill slope so as to maintain a grip on the ski edge, as in picture 7e. You should be in the same position as you started, only one step further up the hill. Now repeat these steps until you are up the hill.

7a–e: Sidestepping to right using ski poles.

8c

Special tips

● If you are slipping backwards, it is because your ski tails are lower than your ski tips; and vice-versa, when you are sliding forwards, it is because your ski tips are lower than your ski tails.

● This manoeuvre should be practised on both sides, so that you feel equally comfortable climbing to the left and right. It should also be performed both with and without using ski poles (picture sequence 8).

● I have found that closing your eyes for a few steps while climbing helps enormously in enabling the feet to 'feel' the position of being perpendicular to the fall-line.

6 Diagonal sidestepping

This manoeuvre is similar to the previous one, only this time the ski is stepped slightly forward at the same time as you step it up the hill (as shown in pictures 9a–d) so that you are climbing on a diagonal course, rather than straight up the hill. The skis, of course, remain perpendicular to the fall-line even as you climb diagonally.

8b

8a–c: Sidestepping to left without using ski poles.   8a

9a–d: Diagonal sidestepping.   9a

9d

Special tip

● This manoeuvre is especially useful when climbing a relatively steep slope, as it is less tiring than straight climbing.

9b

9c

7 Schussing down the fall-line–lifting tails alternately

Here is a good balance exercise. This manoeuvre is similar to straight schussing down the fall-line. The variation is that you alternately lift the tails of your skis as you schuss down the slope.

Start off in the basic position with your skis facing down the fall-line. Start gliding and, as you pick up speed, lift the tail of one ski (by leaning your weight over the other ski) for a count of two. Place the tail back on the snow, lean on this ski and lift the tail of the other ski for a count of two. Repeat until you automatically stop on the uphill runout.

Schussing down fall-line lifting the right ski.   10a

Schussing down fall-line lifting the left ski.   10b

Special tip

● Try to maintain your balance as you lean over the ski that is on the snow, as in pictures 10a and 10b.

8 Schussing down the fall-line–picking up gloves

This manoeuvre teaches you how to bend down and to relax. Place a few gloves in the snow, just to the sides of the fall-line. Start in the basic position with your skis pointing down the hill. Hold your ski poles without putting your hands through the straps. Now push off and leave your poles behind. As you slide down the hill, bend down and lift each glove as you pass alongside it, as shown in pictures 11a and 11b. Stand up between gloves.

Special tips

● If the practice slope is long enough, try to place at least five gloves in the snow.

● Drop each glove as you stand up.

11a and 11b: Picking up gloves in a straight schuss.   11a

9 Bending under ski pole arches

This is another fine manoeuvre, and is as good for adults to practise as it is for children–although children tend to beat adults at it! Arrange ski poles in a series of arches by placing one pole horizontally through the straps of two vertical poles planted in the snow a metre or so apart, as in pictures 12a and 12b. Stand in the basic position above the ski pole arches and start to slide. As you approach the first arch, flex (bend) your knees, lower your hips and crouch low to the ground so that you pass under the horizontal pole, as in picture 12a. As you pass the arch, rise up, as in picture 12b, and then bend again as you pass under the next horizontal pole.

Special tips

● If there is enough room and you can borrow enough ski poles place four or five arches down the slope.

● Be sure to rise up between the arches.

Bending under ski pole arches while schussing.   12a

11b

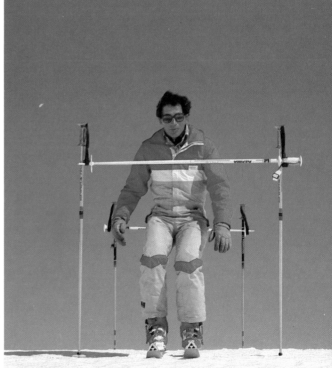

Rising up between ski pole arches while schussing.   12b

Preparation for getting up after a fall; the 'ready' position. **13a**

13b–d: Getting up after a fall. **13b**

10 Getting up after a fall

Everyone falls, and so everyone must get up. But trying to get up incorrectly can be very exhausting and frustrating. Getting up correctly, while not easy in the beginning, soon becomes a habit and is not tiring or difficult once mastered.

When you fall, it is best to try and fall sideways with the skis parallel, as this is the least likely way to get injured. Naturally it is not always possible for you to fall as you would like, but modern release bindings are designed to kick the boot out of the ski in a fall, so it is pretty difficult to injure yourself these days. But it is still preferable to fall sideways if you can.

Having said that, after you fall and are splayed across the snow with legs and arms pointing in all directions, what should you do next? Generally, at the speeds you will be travelling during basic exercises, the skis will remain on when you fall. So the first step is to arrange yourself so that you are sitting with your skis together, perpendicular to the fall-line, and with your body uphill of your skis. Your legs should be bent and your knees tucked up towards your chest. Now, remove your hands from the ski pole grips and place the ski poles in front of your chest with their tips in the snow next to your uphill thigh. Place one hand on top of the grip and the other just above the basket and you will be in the 'ready' position, as

shown in picture 13a. The trick to getting up effortlessly is to lean your chest forward the entire time. Now push upward with your lower hand and simultaneously press down on the top of the grip with your upper hand. If you accompany this action by leaning your torso forward so that your knees are bent towards your chest, you should come up very simply, as in pictures 13b, 13c and 13d.

Special tips

- Due to gravity it is much easier to get up while on a hill than it is while on the flat. The point to remember when on a hill is that the skis must be below you, perpendicular to the fall-line, and when you start to roll up be certain that the edges of the skis bite into the snow so that they do not start to slide away as you lean on them.

- Should your skis come off during the fall, collect them, open the bindings, place the skis perpendicular to the fall-line and stand alongside them. Using your ski poles for support, step into the binding of your lower (downhill) ski and then, standing with your weight on this lower ski, step into the binding of your upper (uphill) ski. If you are on an incline, you should roll your lower ski on to its

13c

13d

uphill edge before stepping on to the uphill ski in order that you don't slide down the incline.

● If you find it too difficult trying to get up with your skis attached, it may prove better to remove your skis and follow the above procedure.

11 The kick turn

There are some ski schools which don't teach this until you are an advanced skier. They believe that it is potentially too dangerous for beginners. My experience is that when taught correctly the kick turn is the easiest and safest way of turning your skis through 180° when standing still on a hill. In all of my years of teaching I have never seen a beginner get hurt performing a properly taught kick turn.

The key to success in the kick turn is to prepare yourself correctly and then to execute the move in three fluid parts. The preparation consists of standing perpendicular to the fall-line, facing downhill. Both the ski poles should be placed in the snow uphill of you, one on either side of your body, and you should lean on these poles, as in picture 14a. It is very important that you face

downhill with your hands visible in front of you. It is equally important that your top ski is very secure in the snow so that when you put your weight on it, it does not slide forwards or backwards. Once the preparation is completed, the turn can be performed.

Step one (picture 14b): swing (do not lift) the lower ski forward and up, place the ski tail in the snow as far forward as you can and as close to the uphill ski as possible with your knee as straight as possible. If performed correctly you should be well balanced, leaning slightly uphill on the edge of your uphill ski, being supported by the ski poles.

Steps two and three are to be done in tandem, though not hurriedly. Step two (pictures 14c and 14d): lower the tip of the vertical ski and place it perpendicularly across the fall-line next to the upper ski and in the opposite direction. The tail of the lower ski should not have moved. (I call this the 'ballet step', though you don't have to be a Nureyev to do it.) The trick to make the step easy, is to bend your downhill knee and to lean your torso over the bottom or downhill ski as you place the ski on the snow. People who experience difficulty at this point do so because they try to lean backwards rather than forwards. If you lean forwards as suggested, bending the lower knee, it is extremely easy to perform step two and then step three.

Step three (pictures 14e and 14f): lean on the lower ski and bring the uphill ski around and place it parallel and next to the lower ski, completing the kick turn manoeuvre.

Special tip

● Another tip to help you make this turn easily is to keep the ski poles behind you until the last part of the manoeuvre. Many people try to bring the ski pole around before the ski, and end up stepping on the pole. The pole and uphill ski should be swung around together, with the ski being planted first followed by the pole.

To summarize, the kick turn is performed as follows: **preparation; step 1**–swing lower leg up and plant ski tail forward and close to uphill ski; **step 2**–leave tail in place, lower the tip of vertical ski, bend the knee, place the ski alongside uphill ski in the opposite direction, and lean out from the waist over the downhill ski; **step 3**–bring uphill ski around, followed closely by ski pole.

Kick turn: Step 1.   14b

Kick turn: Step 2.   14c

Kick turn: Step 2 (continued).   14d

Kick turn: Preparation.   14a

Kick turn: Step 3.   14e

12   The herringbone climb

The herringbone climb is a means of climbing straight up a fairly gentle hill, by walking the skis up the slope in a 'wishbone' fashion. This is performed by leaning against the fronts of the boots, keeping the tails of the skis close together and spreading the ski tips apart. As you step up the hill you plant the ski on its inner edge in order to get a good grip in the snow so as to not slide backwards, as shown in picture 15a. When you have all your weight on this ski, you step the other ski farther up the hill, again with the tip pointing away from the fall-line and step on to this inner edge to get a grip in the snow (picture 15b). This is then repeated as you progress up the hill. This manoeuvre can be performed with and without the use of ski poles.

Note

□ Apart from learning to climb up a hill, the herringbone climb is a useful exercise because it teaches you how to set your ski edges, push off these edges and shift your weight from ski to ski as you walk up the hill. This is very similar to the body movements required for the skating exercises in Day 2.

15b

Kick turn: Step 3 (continued).   14f   15a and 15b: Herringbone climb.   15a

13 The snowplough stop (wedge)

The snowplough or wedge is a means of slowing down or stopping on a gentle gradient at slow speeds. Though some of the modern ski schools no longer teach this movement to beginners, most of the national ski schools still do. I personally feel that the snowplough is a very valuable ski manoeuvre for intermediate and advanced skiers, but is potentially dangerous for beginners to perform. It gives them a false sense of confidence, making them believe that they can stop when they lose control and are going too fast. As the knees are in a twisted position in the snowplough, using this movement at high speeds can put too much stress on the legs and knees, and a fall can result in spiral leg fractures or ligament tears. Furthermore, when beginners lose control they tend to lean backwards, which further aggravates the situation. Consequently, I delay teaching the wedge to those beginners who plan to ski with me for a full five day programme until after day three. By carefully choosing the terrain, I avoid placing my students in situations where they need to employ the snowplough to stop. In the afternoon of Day 1 of the TIP you will learn to stop by stepping the skis towards the hill, which is a graceful movement leading directly to the more advanced manoeuvres.

However, since this book is designed to help you if you are teaching yourself, and as you may find yourself in situations when it would be useful to have such a means of slowing up or stopping, I am including the snowplough (wedge) in the basic exercises. It is very important to remember that this movement should only be performed by beginners on *gentle* slopes at *slow* speeds. (Should you begin to lose control and start skiing too fast, it is preferable to fall sideways, swing your skis below you, and use the ski edges to bite into the snow to slow you to a stop.)

To perform the snowplough or wedge, choose a smooth, gentle slope with an uphill runout at the end. Face down the fall-line in the basic body position as described on page 21 and allow your skis to slide (picture 16a). Be sure to press your shins against the front of your ski boots throughout the entire manoeuvre. As you gain momentum, roll your knees and ankles towards each other and, keeping the ski tips fairly close together, begin to lower your hips and push your feet outwards (picture 16b). Try to keep your weight equally distributed over both feet as you press down, with your upper body balanced midway between the skis. Continue pushing outwards until your skis form a 'V' and you stop (picture 16c).

It is advisable to practise the snowplough (wedge) first on the flat, and 'walk' the skis to the side until you are in the wedge position, as shown in picture 16c. Keep practising on the flat until you feel completely comfortable with the final stopping position before trying it on the gentle slopes.

***

Special tips

● Your weight should be over the *middle* of both ski boots as your skis are on their inner edges (not on the heels).

● Continually lean your shins against the fronts of the ski boots.

● As you push the skis apart, keep your knees and ankles rolled towards each other so that you cause the edges of the skis to dig into the snow. Be sure to keep the tips of the skis close together (about 5–7 cm/2–3 in apart only, as shown in picture 16c), so that your skis are angled, rather than parallel to each other.

● Your upper body should be upright and relaxed the entire time, with your head centred and your arms held in the 'tray holding' position with your ski poles pointed backwards.

***

Having successfully completed all these exercises you should now feel much more comfortable on your skis and should be capable of controlling them at slow speeds. You are now ready to learn the manoeuvres that will allow you to ski in control at higher speeds and on steeper slopes.

16a–c: Snowplough stop (wedge).

16a

16c

16b

Traverse

(Day 1 Afternoon)

The purpose of these exercises is:

- To learn to maintain the correct body position while skiing across a slope.

- To learn to control and steer the downhill ski.

- To learn to use the edges of the skis.

- To learn to shift your weight from ski to ski.

- To learn to change direction and stop.

A skier is in the traverse position 98 per cent of the time. It is the position you are in when skiing across a slope, and the position you are in before and after a turn. The only time you are not in a traverse position is when skiing the fall-line in a straight schuss position – and this is normally only done at the bottom or runout of a slope.

Since many runs are cut *across* the fall-line, even when skiing straight down the run without turning, the skier is generally not on the fall-line and therefore must assume the traverse position. My experience is that if you learn the correct traverse position as early as possible you will make the greatest progress and therefore, unlike other ski teaching systems, TIP teaches this movement on the first day. My biggest difficulty in teaching students who come to me as intermediate skiers wanting to improve, is correcting their basic traverse position. Usually these intermediate skiers display too much body movement and often swing their hips, bend from their waists or throw their arms around, upsetting their balance. I therefore have to spend a great deal of time on corrective exercises rather than on progressive exercises.

When executed correctly, the traverse position is very easy and requires remarkably little movement of the parts of your body.

These exercises are to be performed on a gentle hill (beginners' slope)

1   The basic traverse position

As can be seen in picture 17, rather than facing the skis straight down the fall-line as in the straight schuss position, the skis are pointed across the fall-line. The speed of descent is determined by whether the skis are pointing closest to the perpendicular to the fall-line or to the fall-line itself. Naturally the position closest to the perpendicular – called a 'shallow' traverse – will cause the slowest descent, and that closest to the fall-line – called a 'steep' traverse – will be the fastest descent in traverse. Whenever the skis are across the fall-line (shallow, steep or any stage in between), your body should be in the traverse position.

To assume the traverse position, as shown in picture 17, all the uphill parts of your body should be slightly in front of their downhill counterparts. To achieve this, I like to go through a checklist, working from the skis up to the head.

Start with the skis about 5–12 cm (2–5 in) apart and extend the uphill ski forward about a quarter to a half of a boot length. (The uphill foot is now automatically in front of the downhill foot, and the uphill knee is automatically in front of the downhill knee.) Now twist your body slightly so that the uphill side of your hip is in front of the downhill side, and turn your shoulders so that the uphill shoulder is slightly in front of the downhill shoulder. Your body should therefore be facing slightly downhill. Your head should be relaxed and centred, and facing the direction of the traverse, so that when you start to ski you can see where you are going. Your arms should be held still, as though you are carrying a tray. Your ski poles should be held at your sides pointing slightly backwards. The next requirements are very important in order to control the skis.

Press your shins against the fronts of the ski boots so that you have a space between the calf muscles and the backs of the ski boots. Your top buckle should not be so tight as to prevent you from leaning comfortably against the front of your boot, nor so loose that you have no support. Modern boots, made of strong plastic, support the body well and help prevent muscle pains. Skiers who suffer from painful shins are those who do not continually lean against the fronts of their boots but rather bang against them as they try to lean forward to regain control.

Next, incline your knees and ankles towards the uphill slope so that your skis are no longer flat on the snow but are making contact on their uphill edges. Lastly, lean your body so that your weight is predominately over your downhill ski. Your torso should be naturally upright and relaxed. Your knees should be relaxed and bent just enough so that you are in a slightly crouched position, with the centre of gravity of your body over the middle of your downhill ski boot.

Special tips

- This is the normal traverse position for skiing on packed snow. When skiing on icy snow the centre of gravity must be brought forward over the ball of the downhill foot–this is accomplished by leaning your upper body further forward over the downhill ski. When skiing in deeper snow, the centre of gravity should be over the heels–this is accomplished by sitting just a little lower and keeping your torso upright. Skiing on ice and in powder snow are advanced skiing manoeuvres, and are explained in greater detail in Sections Two and Three. When learning the traverse position, it is best to be on packed snow.

- When skiing on steeper slopes modify the basic traverse position by rolling the knees and ankles slightly more uphill (thereby 'edging' the skis more) and leaning the upper body more downhill.

2 Shallow traverse–lifting tail of uphill ski

Start in a traverse position close to the perpendicular to the fall-line and push off with your ski poles. While traversing across the slope, lift the tail of your uphill ski, as in picture 18. This is accomplished by leaning over the downhill ski in order to take your weight off the uphill ski. (If

you are leaning on the uphill ski you cannot lift the tail.) Hold the ski tail in the air for a count of three and then place it back alongside the downhill ski. As you are in a shallow traverse, you will stop as you lose momentum.

Repeat this manoeuvre in the opposite direction and practise lifting the other ski. Most people find this easier on one side than on the other, so be certain to work on the less favourable side since skiing requires equal balance and control in both directions.

Traverse position.   17

Lifting tail of uphill ski in traverse.   18

3 Shallow traverse–touching bottom of downhill ski boot

Start as in the previous exercise and, while moving, lean over and touch the bottom of the downhill ski boot just where the arch of the boot comes in contact with the ski (picture 19). Hold this position for a count of three and then stand up again, assuming a good traverse position. Repeat in the opposite direction.

Special tips

● The trick here is to incline the downhill knee more towards the hill, making it easier to lean over sideways.

● This is an excellent exercise to 'feel' how to ride on the uphill edge of the downhill ski.

4 Shallow traverse–holding ski poles across chest

Hold your ski poles horizontally in front of your chest with the palms downwards and with one hand just below the grips and the other just above the baskets, as in picture 20. Since your chest is facing downhill, the ski poles are across the fall-line. Traverse across the slope in this position.

This exercise can also be done lifting the tail of the uphill ski as a means of combining this and exercise 2. Repeat in the opposite direction.

Note

☐ I have found that this is a very good corrective exercise for intermediate and advanced skiers with incorrect traverse positions. I therefore recommend that all intermediate and advanced skiers execute this manoeuvre in both directions to ascertain whether or not they have a flawless traverse position.

Touching downhill ski boot while traversing.   19

Holding ski poles across chest while traversing.   20

5 Shallow traverse–alternately lifting tail and touching boot

As you traverse across the slope, hold the tail of the uphill ski in the air for a count of three, and then traverse with both skis in the snow for a count of three. Now bend down and touch the downhill ski boot for a count of three and then stand up and finish by traversing to a stop. Repeat on the opposite side.

6 Stepping uphill to stop

While you are skiing on a shallow traverse you will not have to worry about stopping, as you will run out of momentum naturally. But when you start performing these manoeuvres on steeper traverses it will be necessary to have a means of stopping in order to prevent yourself from going off the side of the run. This stepping uphill manoeuvre not only teaches the proper use of the edges as well as how to shift the weight from one ski to the other, but also allows you to slow up or stop by stepping your skis up the hill into a shallower traverse until you stop naturally.

This manoeuvre should be practised first on the flat, then on a gentle slope while standing still, then on a shallow traverse using a small push of the ski poles to get you into a very slow glide, then with a longer glide and finally, after a complete traverse across the slope.

Note

□ When performing this on the flat your body should 'realize' that this manoeuvre is essentially the same as the Beginner Exercise 'turning in position using the tails as a pivot', the difference while gliding being that you have to maintain your balance on one ski at a time while you are moving.

To perform the stopping manoeuvre from a slow glide, start in a traverse position on a shallow traverse with your weight on your downhill ski (picture 21a). Push off with your ski poles so that you start to glide slowly. During the glide lift the shovel of your uphill ski and step this ski slightly up the hill, leading with the ski tip, as in picture 21b. Place the ski on the snow and lean on the uphill edge (to prevent the ski from sliding sideways)–picture 21c. Maintain your traverse position with your uphill shoulder and hip in front of the downhill counterparts so that your body is still facing downhill. (You must resist the tendency to twist your body in the direction you are stepping.) The weight is now on the uphill ski. Now bring the downhill ski parallel to the uphill ski and once more put your weight on the downhill ski (picture 21d). You will now be in a traverse position on a shallower traverse. If you are still going too fast the procedure should be repeated until you are on a traverse that will permit your skis to stop naturally. Repeat in the opposite direction.

Special tips

● Remember to practise this manoeuvre first on the flat, and then on a slope while standing still. After practising with a short glide, increase your speed and length of glide.

● Your shins should be leaning against the fronts of the boots throughout this exercise, your knees should be relaxed, the uphill knee, hip, shoulder and arm should be leading, and your weight should be carried over the arch of the ski boots.

● The trick to this manoeuvre is to leave the tails of the skis in place when stepping the skis up the hill. If you lift the whole ski and place it a full step up the hill in a parallel traverse direction to the one you are in, you will not slow down.

● If you take *small* steps and don't hurry the movements you will find it easy to perform this manoeuvre. My experience is that people want to slow down too quickly and consequently try to take a large, abrupt step up the hill which inevitably leads to a fall while doing 'the splits'.

● Try to be graceful and allow the skis to glide as you are making small steps.

21b

21a

21a–d: Stepping uphill to stop (see previous page).

21d

21c

22a

7 Traverse, touch boot and step uphill to stop

You are now ready to apply what you have so far learnt. Start in a medium traverse and push off with the ski poles (picture sequence 22). While gliding, bend down and touch your downhill ski boot and then stand up and continue gliding in the same traverse. When you are midway across the slope step the skis up the hill and glide to a stop. Repeat in the opposite direction.

22d

22b

22c

22e

22a–e: Touching boot and stepping uphill to stop while traversing.

8 Steeper traverse exercises

Now that you can safely and confidently step to a stop to both sides, all the traverse exercises (2–7) should be performed on a steeper traverse path, in other words, closer to the fall-line. As your confidence grows you should increase the steepness of the direction until you are starting just off the fall-line. Referring to fig 1 you should begin each exercise in traverse A, a shallow traverse, close to the perpendicular to the fall-line; then repeat in traverse B, a slightly steeper traverse, closer to the fall-line; then in traverse C, D and E, each traverse becoming steeper and closer to the fall-line.

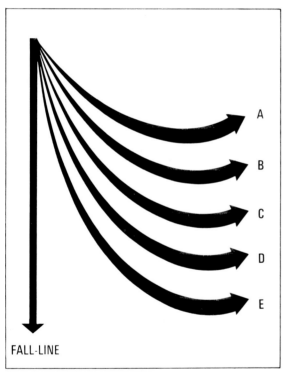

Fig 1   Start exercises in shallow traverse (A) and increase the steepness until you are starting just off the fall-line.

Hopefully you have become aware that all the manoeuvres described so far have been done with your lower body. Your upper body has done little except to remain relaxed, and has been used only to maintain your balance over the instep of either your downhill or uphill ski. As you progress to more advanced manoeuvres you will find this still to be the case. Skiers who use their upper body too much tend to throw themselves off balance and are constantly seeking to regain their balance. I prefer a relatively 'quiet' or 'still' upper body for most ski manoeuvres. You are now at the end of Day 1 and should be feeling much more confident on your skis. Your skis and boots should be feeling less alien, and you should be starting to enjoy the new sensations of gliding movement on the snow.

For the less athletic among you, there is nothing wrong with continuing to practise the Beginner Exercises and Traverse the entire first day and second morning, and start your Sidesliding on the second afternoon. You should still be making nice parallel turns on the fifth day and, by spending more time on the basics, you will make better progress throughout the week than if you proceed too quickly. You must be honest with yourself about your athletic ability, however, and if you have never been very good at sports there is no reason to believe that you will be able instantly to be a skiing superstar. But the nice thing about skiing as a recreational sport is that it is non-competitive and you can go at your own pace. I have never seen a determined person fail to learn to ski! In fact, over the years I have taught a number of severely disabled persons to learn to ski and, as far as I know, they are still skiing and enjoying their holidays, skiing confidently and safely at their own pace.

For those of you who are reasonably athletic, you should at this point be eager to move on to the sidesliding and skating manoeuvres that are awaiting you on Day 2.

Sidesliding

(Day 2 Morning)

The purpose of these exercises is:

- To learn how to correctly use the ski edges for sidesliding and control.

- To learn to use the knees and ankles to control the amount of edging required to cause the skis to either grip in the snow or to make them slide sideways.

- To reinforce the traverse position while sidesliding.

- To teach your body the subtlety of lower body movement required for the transition from traversing to sidesliding.

All the sidesliding exercises should be performed on a short, steep slope

---

1 Sidesliding–pushing with ski poles

Start in a traverse position with your skis perpendicular to the fall-line and with both ski poles planted in the snow uphill (similar to the start of the kick turn). Your upper body should be facing straight down the fall-line. Place the ski poles close to the skis (picture 23a) and start pushing the poles backwards. Release your ski edges slightly by rolling your knees and ankles in the downhill direction. Maintain your skis perpendicular to the fall-line as you are pushing on your poles, and allow the skis to slip gently sideways down the fall-line as in picture 23b. When your hands are fully extended behind you, as in picture 23c, bring the ski poles back to the original position close to the skis and again push them away from you.

Repeat this manoeuvre facing in the opposite direction.

Special tips

- The trick to this manoeuvre is not to roll your knees and ankles too far downhill or you will catch the downhill edge and fall over it.

- Try to maintain your proper traverse position with your weight over your downhill ski.

- Notice in pictures 23a, 23b, and 23c that the knees are relaxed and the shins are leaning on the fronts of the ski boots.

23a

23b

23a–c: Sidesliding–pushing with ski poles. 23c

2   Sidesliding–one foot at a time

Start in a traverse position with your weight on the instep of the downhill ski boot, the shins against the fronts of the ski boots and your arms and ski poles held comfortably in the 'tray-carrying' position, with the elbows bent for balance. Push the downhill ski down the fall-line, keeping the ski perpendicular to the fall-line.

(Your weight will shift to your uphill ski.) When your ski is extended to a point well before you do the splits, get a good grip with the edge biting into the snow, transfer your weight back on to this edge and slide the uphill ski alongside the lower ski. Again, push your downhill ski down the fall-line and bring the uphill ski alongside. Continue these movements until you feel comfortable and in control of your skis, and then repeat in the opposite direction.

24a

24b

24a–c: Straight sidesliding down fall-line.

24c

3   Straight sidesliding

Assume a proper traverse position with your
arms in the 'tray carrying' position for balance.
Keep your weight on the instep of your downhill
ski boot and roll your knees and ankles downhill
(picture 24a). Your skis, as they start to flatten,
will begin to slide down the fall-line (picture
24b). Try to control the slide so that the skis
remain perpendicular to the fall-line as they are
sliding. When you are ready to stop, roll your
knees and ankles uphill again and your edges will
begin to dig into the snow (picture 24c).

Special tip

● The tricks here are to constantly maintain shin
  contact with the fronts of the ski boots, to keep
  your weight on the downhill ski and not to
  overroll your ankles and knees. (You don't
  want the skis totally flat on the snow or you
  will fall over the downhill edge.)

Notes

□ On wet, sticky snow, it is necessary to wax the
  skis so that they slide easily. Almost every ski
  shop has a hotwaxing machine that can wax
  your skis for the prevailing snow conditions
  and it is a good idea to bring your skis in and
  have them properly prepared. Properly
  waxed skis are safer than skis that stick to the
  snow as they react quicker to your movements
  and will respond as directed. Skis that stick
  will often cause you to fall at slow speeds,
  which can be potentially dangerous. Furthermore, sidesliding is difficult with sticky skis, as
  the snow gathers under them.

□ This exercise teaches the nuance of movement
  required to start the skis sliding.

Picture sequence 25 shows a close-up of the
ankles and knees during the sidesliding movement. Notice how the skis flatten when the knees
and ankles are rolled downhill (which starts the
skis sliding) and how the skis are edged when the
knees and ankles are rolled back uphill to stop the
slide.

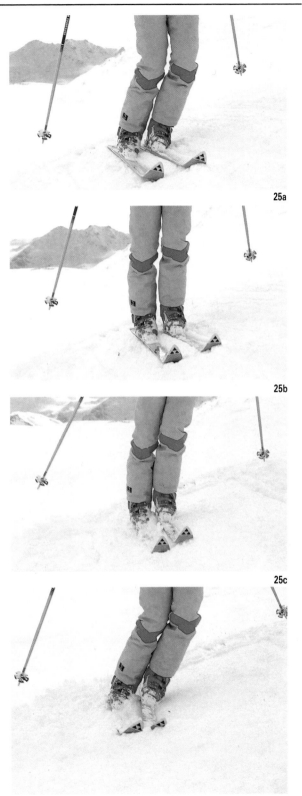

25a

25b

25c

25a–d: Close-up of knees and ankles when sidesliding. 25d

4 Diagonal sidesliding

I find that many people have trouble with this manoeuvre when they try mentally to force themselves to slide down the hill sideways and go forward at the same time, so I use a little trick which almost never fails. Instead of thinking of diagonal sidesliding as a separate manoeuvre, think of it as *traversing* to a point on the other side of the slope with your *skis flattened a little*. (It is actually easier to sideslide than to traverse, since during sidesliding you do not have to put as much pressure on the edges as you do when traversing.)

26a

26b

26a–c: Diagonal sidesliding across a hill.

26c

To perform this manoeuvre, assume a proper traverse position. While standing still, roll your ankles and knees downhill (just enough so the skis are still on their edges but almost flat on the snow). Now when you try to traverse, because your skis are less edged, they will slide downhill as you are moving forward. In pictures 26a–26c, you see the diagonal track being engraved in the snow during a diagonal sideslide.

Special tips

● Keep your eye on the point you've chosen across the slope (a run marker, a tree, a lift tower) and try to keep your ski tips pointed towards this object as you descend. This will help prevent your skis from running away down the hill.

● Be sure to maintain a gentle, constant pressure on the front of your ski boots with a gap between your calf muscles and the backs of the ski boots, otherwise your weight will tilt backwards and you will have trouble controlling your skis.

● Throughout the manoeuvre your weight should be over the instep of your downhill ski boot.

● Try to keep your upper body still.

---

5 Staircase sidesliding

This is one of my favourite exercises. It also brings back fond memories, as it is similar to the sidesliding exercise that I was called upon to demonstrate when I took my certification course, and it has remained a constant feature in my teaching through all the years of experimentation and innovation. I especially like this manoeuvre because it teaches the subtlety of ankle and knee movement and gives beginners great confidence on their skis as a consequence of the control that they learn to acquire. I also like this manoeuvre because it is extremely useful when skiing a narrow run that is on a bias to the fall-line, especially when skiing in crowds.

Staircase sidesliding is nothing more than a combination of straight sidesliding and traverse, both of which you have already performed. It is called staircase sidesliding, not surprisingly, because the track in the snow resembles a staircase, as can be seen in picture 27e.

To perform this manoeuvre, traverse across an intermediate grade slope, as shown in picture 27a. After going some 2 to 3 metres (6 to 10 ft), roll your ankles and knees downhill and, without stopping, begin to sideslide (picture 27b). Continue to sideslide for approximately 1 to 1.5 metres (3 to 5 ft), and then roll your ankles and knees towards the hill and press your downhill ski edges into the snow (picture 27c). Without stopping, and with your knees rolled towards the hill, traverse again for some 2 to 3 metres (6 to 10 ft)–picture 27d.

Continue to repeat these alternating movements until you have crossed the slope. Repeat the manoeuvre in the opposite direction.

Special tip

● To test your capability, sideslide diagonally rather than straight every other traverse, and try to perform this manoeuvre very slowly.

Notes

☐ Whenever I have intermediate and advanced skiers wanting to improve, but who tend to make too many movements with their upper bodies, I have them perform this exercise at very slow speeds. It always amazes them that they find it difficult to do.

☐ Quite often skiers get into the bad habit of throwing their hips to turn their skis, and often lose–or never establish–the sensitive contact between their feet and the snow. This exercise is designed to establish that contact.

27a

27b

27a–d: Staircase sidesliding.

27c

27d

Staircase sidesliding—showing staircase track in snow.   27e

☐ You will find sidesliding to be a very useful manoeuvre when you start to ski the runs on mountains, for whenever you encounter a pitch on a slope that you feel is too steep to ski, too narrow to allow you to confidently make turns, or too icy or rocky, you can always sideslide safely. No matter how advanced a skier you become you will always encounter places where you must sideslide. Therefore, learn to sideslide confidently and you will always have a safety manoeuvre when needed.

You have now learned the two most important safety manoeuvres; sidesliding for beginner and intermediate skiers, and the kick turn for advanced skiers. I have lost count of the number of times I have led advanced skiers off the packed slopes into the back-bowls and have come to a place where for one reason or other we have had to turn around to get down another way, only to be told that they cannot kick turn. Thus they have had to walk backwards along treacherous cliffs in order to find room to turn around. I now make skiers demonstrate to me the kick turn before I take them off the slopes. So, as beginners, I recommend that you go back and practise your kick turn now until it is as easy to do as signing your name. Similarly, practise sidesliding when ever you can, so that these techniques are ready to be used when needed.

Skating and learning to ride ski-lifts

(Day 2 Afternoon)

The purpose of these exercises is:

● To learn how to shift your weight from one ski to the other.

● To help achieve better balance.

● To practise the down-up-down movements or, as the French call it, 'flexion-extension-flexion'.

● To gain a better understanding of the use of the ski edges.

● To learn to change direction while moving.

● To practise independent action of the legs.

● To learn to ride ski-lifts.

'Skating' is a ski manoeuvre that many ski schools do not teach to adults, but only include in their teaching curriculum for children. This, I feel, is a serious mistake, as skating is one of the most beneficial skiing manoeuvres to help anyone's body feel comfortable and relaxed on skis. While skating, the ankles and knees are being taught the same movements used for the parallel turn, the legs and hips are taught the down-up-down movements which will later be translated into up-unweighting, and the body is trained to shift its weight from ski to ski and learns how to change direction easily while moving. Skating also helps to improve a skier's balance.

I have always observed that at the end of the skating exercises students feel very familiar and at ease with their skis and consequently make excellent progress in the subsequent skiing manoeuvres. I therefore recommend that all beginners and intermediate skiers who are not comfortable skating spend the time necessary to practise all the exercises in this section.

Note

□ It is best to practise the basic skating movements on the flat and then, when they are learnt, practise the gliding exercises on a gentle slope. Start with very little exaggeration of body movement. When you begin to 'feel' the skating movements, exaggerate the down-up-down leg thrusts. As you become more advanced you will find that eventually you will be able to skate even on the more difficult slopes.

1 Skating on the flat

This manoeuvre should be performed first with very little exaggeration of body movements and then with more exaggerated body movements, and should be thought of as roller skating or ice skating with longer blades. Refer to pictures 28a–d. Spread the tips of the skis slightly apart so that the ski tails are closer together than the ski tips. Now 'set' the edge of one ski by rolling the knee and ankle of that leg inward. Push off with that ski and glide on the other ski. While gliding, roll the knees and ankle of this leg inward, set the edge, and push off on the other ski. Do at least four or five of these skating manoeuvres.

Special tips

● You will find that if you do not roll your knee and ankle inward, the ski will remain flat on the snow and when you push off the edge, the ski will slide away. Therefore, it is necessary to 'set' that edge so that you have a firm grip when you push off.

● The other trick to this manoeuvre is, after you push off, to lean out over the gliding ski (as in pictures 28d and 29b) so that you don't find yourself caught between the skis. (Your body should be moving from side to side as you push and glide.)

28a

28b

28c

28d

28a–d: Skating on the flat–shifting weight from ski to ski with minimal knee bending.

29a

29b

29a and 29b: Skating on the flat–shifting weight from ski to ski with exaggerated body movements (deep knee bend and hard leg thrust); also showing body leaning out over the gliding ski and the track left in the snow by the firm edge set.

These exercises should be performed on a gentle slope

2   Skating down the fall-line–skating as a 'fencing' manoeuvre

The motion required is the same as skating on the flat, only now you will have more gliding speed and the setting of the edges will require more precision.

At this point, I should like to point out that there is a great similarity of body movements in different sports. This is natural, since the body is only capable of just so many movements. It is as well to realize that although you are in a new medium using different equipment, the actual body movements required have already been learnt via some other activity. The traverse position for instance is similar to a backhand position in tennis. Likewise, skating is similar to fencing. As you can see in pictures 30a and 30b, if you hold your ski poles like you would a fencing foil and imagine your opponent up the hill from you, in order to thrust at him you must bend your lower leg, point your upper leg (and ski), push off the lower leg (downhill ski) and lean over the thrusting leg (uphill ski). As on a flat surface, and even more so on a slope, it is necessary to set the edge of the downhill ski so that you have a firm grip from which to push off.

30c

30a

30a and 30b: Skating as a 'fencing' manoeuvre. 30b

If you now hold your ski poles in the normal fashion, as in pictures 30c and 30d, and perform exactly the same movement as the fencing thrust, you will find skating easy.

30c and 30d: Skating with hard edge set and with 30d exaggerated thrust movement, showing good body lean on thrusting (or gliding) ski.

On a gentle beginners' slope with an uphill or flat runout, skate a path down the fall-line. Start with little exaggeration and then exaggerate the bending and thrusting movements. Concentrate on setting your edges and shifting your weight from ski to ski.

Special tips

- As you are gliding, start to lower your body as you roll your knee and ankle inwards, so that you can get a hard edge set when you are ready to thrust in the new direction.

- When you are moving quickly, it is best to lift the stepping ski so that the tail is slightly higher than the tip (as in picture 30c) and cross it over the pushing ski, keeping the boots fairly close together. Now place the stepping ski in the snow with the tip first, followed smoothly by the rest of the ski as your body weight transfers to this ski during the glide.

31b

31a

31d

31c

31a–d: Skating to the right during traverse with exaggerated bending and thrusting.

3   Skating uphill

I recommend that you briefly repeat the step turn uphill which was practised during Traverse (page 39). This manoeuvre is nothing more than half a skating step. (In this movement one ski becomes the stepping and gliding ski while the other remains the pushing ski.) Having already practised skating from one ski to the other you should find this exercise easy to do and should try to exaggerate the bending and thrusting (flexion-extension-flexion) movements as you 'half-step' your skis to a stop, as shown in pictures 31a–31d).

4   Skating to a stop

This manoeuvre is simply a combination of skating down the fall-line and then skating uphill to a stop. Start by facing down the fall-line and begin skating from side to side down the fall-line. When you have done four or five skating steps

start leaning in one direction and skate to a stop with a number of small half-steps up the slope away from the fall-line. Repeat this exercise and skate to a stop in the opposite direction.

5   Skating across the fall-line

This and the next exercise will determine how comfortably you are skating and whether you have mastered the use of your ski edges. Refer to fig 2. Start by skating down the fall-line and after two or three skating steps start half-skating to one side. Instead of skating to a stop, however, start to half-skate *down* the hill to the opposite side so that you are having to turn across the fall-line. Your stepping/gliding ski now becomes your pushing ski, and vice-versa.

After crossing the fall-line, again change your stepping/gliding ski and pushing ski and half-skate downhill across the fall-line so that you are making a series of skating turns down the hill.

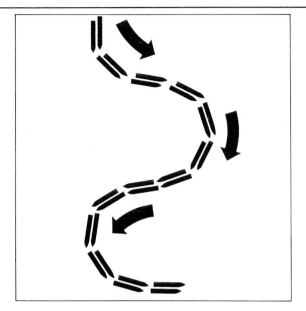

Fig 2. Skating a series of turns down the slope.

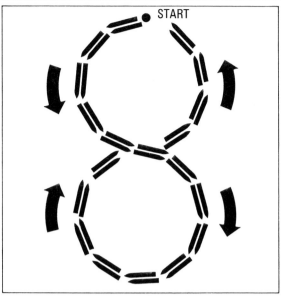

Fig 3. Skating a figure-of-eight on a very gentle slope.

Special tips

● The trick to this manoeuvre is to be certain to lean your body in the direction you are heading so that it will be over the leading ski, especially as you change direction.

● A further trick is to lead with the *knee* that is in the direction you wish to head.

Special tip

● The uphill part of the figure-of-eight requires strong leg thrusts and speed when changing direction. As in the previous exercise, lead with the knee that is in the direction you want to head, and lean the upper body well forward and over the gliding ski (pictures 32d, 32e and 32f). (Naturally there will not be too much glide as you push uphill.)

6   Skating a figure-of-eight

Perform this, the culmination of skating manoeuvres, on a very gentle slope, as part of the manoeuvre will require you to ski uphill. Refer to fig 3 and picture sequence 32. Start in a traverse position to the right, and half-skate across the fall-line to the left and then, after crossing the fall-line, half-skate to the right as you proceed down the hill. So far, this is the same as the previous manoeuvre. Now comes the demanding part as, instead of continuing to skate downhill across the fall-line, you must continue half-skating *up the hill*, completing a circle, crossing your track at midpoint and then, changing directions, continue half-skating uphill until you are at your starting point, completing the figure-of-eight.

Skiing a figure-of-eight is a 'fun manoeuvre' and not absolutely necessary for everyone to perform; but if you are strong and able and want to see how well you have mastered skating, give it a try.

7   Riding a ski-lift

Whether you've performed the figure-of-eight or not, you should be feeling very much more at ease on your skis than before, and should be finding it easy to control and steer your skis. You are therefore ready to ride the ski-lifts safely up the mountains.

Depending on the facilities at your ski area you may find that to get to the slope on which you

32a-h: Figure-of-eight on a very gentle slope.

wish to train you will have to ride a mechanical ski-lift up the mountain. If the lift is a 'tramway'—a large box-shaped cabin (picture 33a), or a 'gondola'—an egg-shaped bubble or cube (pictures 33b and 33c), consider yourself lucky as these whisk you up the mountain and unload you without having your skis attached; in other words, you carry your skis with you or put them in a ski rack attached to the lift. If you have a chair-lift (picture 33d), again the uphill ride will be easy. The correct way to ride a chair-lift is to align yourself properly at the entry as indicated by the attendant, and wait for the chair to come around the wheel while looking over your shoulder so that you watch the chair approach. Remove your ski poles from your wrist and hold them in one hand. Use the other hand to guide the chair under you and sit down as the chair moves beneath you. If your chair has a safety bar, close the bar once you've settled into the seat. If you are riding a two-person chair hold your ski poles towards the outside while waiting for the chair. Three- and four-person chairs require you to take more care with your ski poles so that you do not interfere with others getting on the same chair.

Before getting to the top of the hill there should be a notice telling you to raise the safety bar. You should therefore lift your feet from the foot rest (not all chair-lifts have foot rests), open the bar and be ready to get off the chair when you reach the exit ramp. When you arrive at the exit ramp there will often be a sign indicating where you should stand up. So lean forward in the chair, place your skis on the snow, stand up and ski down the exit ramp. To stop, you can easily step or skate uphill.

Special tip

● It is best to move away from the unloading area as soon as possible so as to allow the next person to unload safely.

In most European ski areas the beginners' slopes are serviced by either a Poma lift (sometimes called a button lift, a disk-pull lift, or a drag lift)–picture 33e; or a T-bar lift–picture 33f. Both of these lifts pull you up the slope with your skis attached and riding on the snow. The Poma lifts seem to be more common in France, and the T-bars more common in Austria and Switzerland (and Chile). North American resorts favour chair-lifts, although many of the smaller areas have a mixture of T-bars and Poma lifts.

When riding either of these types of ski-lifts the key is to *stand up*, leaning against the fronts of your ski boots with your knees relaxed and allow the lift to pull you up the hill. For both of these types of ski-lifts, you should remove your ski pole straps from your wrists and carry the ski poles in your free hand.

The Poma lift goes between your legs and you hold on to the bar that moves along a cable as the disk pulls you up the hill. The T-bar is meant to be ridden by two persons (though it can also be ridden by one), and you hold on to the vertical bar that is between you and your partner as the horizontal bar that is placed behind your thighs pulls you up the mountain. When getting on to a T-bar, hold your ski poles in your outside hand and look over your inside shoulder (the shoulder closest to your partner) so that you can see the

bar approaching, and then grip the vertical bar as it passes between you and your partner.

Note

□ In Australia the lift operators are very keen that you hold your ski poles 'tips forward', so that you do not stab them as they help load you on to the lift. This is wise to do whenever there are attendant-operated lifts.

As both of these lifts are on spring tensions, if you sit on them the spring will expand and you will find yourself sitting on the snow as you are being pulled up the hill. Should this happen it is best to let go, scramble out of the track, get up, and then walk or skate down to the start and begin again. Depending on the steepness of the slope alongside the lift, it may be preferable to remove your skis and carry them down to the start. While riding these lifts you should keep your feet spaced apart so that your skis are riding in the grooves made by previous skiers. Watch that your tips do not cross. When you arrive at the top of the hill there should be a sign indicating where you should release the bar and often there is an arrow indicating the direction to ski away. At this point you pull down on the bar, pull it out from between your legs (in the case of the Poma lift) and push it away as you maintain your momentum and ski in the direction that the arrow indicates. Once you have stopped, walk or ski out of the unloading area to allow a clear exit for the next skiers. When you are safely away from the unloading area you can put your ski poles on and then you will be ready to enjoy the descent down the slope.

Note

□ It is preferable to delay learning to ride the ski-lifts until after the skating lesson because at this point you are more relaxed and more aware of how to control your skis. In certain areas, due to the location of the gentle slopes, it may be more practical to learn to ride the lifts sooner and you can do so at any time subsequent to the Beginner Exercises; however, my experience is that the later it is done the safer and more efficient it will be.

Tramway. 33a

Gondola. 33b

Gondola. 33c

Chair-lift. 33d

Poma lift. 33e

T-bar lift. 33f

Uphill turns
(parallel turns uphill) and an explanation of why skis turn

(Day 3 Morning)

The purpose of these exercises is:

- To learn how to use the ankles and knees correctly to keep the skis parallel while gliding and turning.

- To learn how to make the skis turn off a traverse track.

- To learn to parallel ski to a stop.

- To learn to change direction utilizing the ski edges.

- To understand why skis turn.

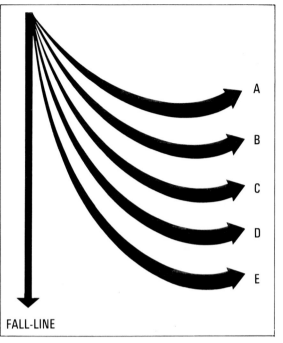

Fig 4. Starting uphill turns on shallow traverse A and increasing steepness of traverse (B, C, D) until E, starting on the fall-line.

These exercises should be performed on a gentle slope

1 Turning the skis uphill to make a stop

The approach for learning uphill turns is similar to the final traverse exercises, in other words, you first perform the manoeuvre in a shallow traverse, and gradually increase the steepness of the traverse until you are starting on the fall-line (see fig 4).

During the traverse exercises, you stopped by stepping your skis up the hill. In this manoeuvre you will glide your skis to a stop, always keeping both skis on the snow and always on their edges. A little ditty that I like to sing to my students and have them repeat is: 'We steer our skis by pressing our knees', with the emphasis on the last word 'knees'. The reason for the emphasis on knees is to help the student focus his or her attention on using the knees rather than the hips or shoulders to direct the skis. The point being, as mentioned

in earlier sections, that you control your skis with your lower body, rather than with your upper body.

A Starting on a shallow traverse

Start on a shallow traverse in a good traverse position on a gentle slope and gather some speed (picture 34a). When you are ready to turn uphill, steer the skis by pressing your knees in the direction you want to go (uphill) as in pictures 34b–34d, and steadily lower your hips so that your weight is pressing down on the instep of your downhill ski boot.

Special tips

- It is very important to be pressing down over the instep of your downhill ski boot as you are making the turn.

- It is also important to lean your shins against the fronts of your ski boots as you steer your knees in the direction of the turn.

34a–d: Turning the skis uphill to stop.   **34d**   **34c**

Note

☐ Notice in picture sequence 34 how the upper body remains still during this manoeuvre. Beginners try to pull themselves around by leaning their upper body in the direction they want to go. That doesn't work! In fact, that is like climbing up a steep hill with slippery shoes; the shoes keep slipping out from under you because there is no friction, in other words, no resistance. The reason you roll your knees up the hill is to put the skis on their edges, and the reason that you must push down on the edge is to force the edge to bite into the snow, thereby creating friction along the edge (hence a resistance between the skis and the snow) which, because of the shape of the skis, causes the skis to turn. By trying to 'pull' yourself around you are taking the weight off the instep of the downhill foot and therefore off the edge of the downhill ski, and the ski will not turn.

Why the skis turn

Although I emphasize learning to ski by 'feeling' the sensations required to perform the various movements, I believe it can be useful if skiers understand why their skis turn.

Obviously you can turn a ski by jumping in the air and landing with your skis in a new direction. When I learnt to ski this was, in fact, the way we turned our skis. We used an exaggerated upward movement which lifted the ski tails off the snow and we jumped the tails across the fall-line, landing with the skis pointing in the new traverse position. Naturally this was somewhat hard on the knees and was quite tiring, for all but the youngest and fittest. As the use of modern technologies became incorporated into modern ski manufacture, so an understanding of ski dynamics became incorporated into the ski design, and the skis that you use today are much more sophisticated than those with which I started.

We are also indebted to the racing circuit since racers and manufacturers were, and still are, constantly seeking ways of making the skis turn more easily in order to give them the advantage over their competitors. These concepts have found their way into our recreational skis, resulting in skis that essentially turn by themselves with very little effort on the part of the skier. No longer do we have to thrust our skis into the air, winding and unwinding our body like a coiled spring in order to turn the skis. All we now have to do is press on the ski edges in a particular manner and the shape of the side of the ski and the energy transmitted to the ski automatically causes it to turn, making skiing as physically easy for older skiers as for youngsters.

To understand the technicalities of why skis turn it is necessary to understand the basic construction of modern skis.

Fig 5 shows a ski on a flat surface.

34b   34a

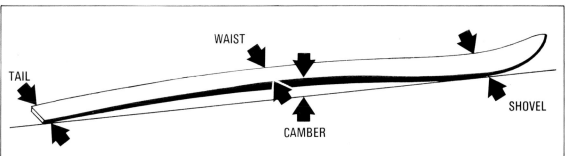

WAIST

TAIL

CAMBER

SHOVEL

Fig 5. The parts of a ski.

Ski camber Notice that the ski does not lie flat on the surface but rather is arched so that only the front and back parts of the ski contact the surface. This feature of a ski is called ski camber. Because of ski camber, when a skier stands over the middle of a ski, his or her weight is distributed along its entire length. Naturally, since the front and back parts of the skis are already in contact with the surface when a ski is unweighted, when a skier stands on the ski the front and back parts are pressed even harder into the snow.

Ski sidecut Notice also in fig 5 that the skis are not evenly broad over their entire length. The skis are widest at the shovel, narrowest at the waist and wide at the tail. This feature is called ski sidecut and, combined with ski camber, is responsible for a ski carving in the snow during a turn.

Because the shovel and tail of a ski are wider than the waist, when you roll your ski on to its edge the contact with the snow at the shovel and

tail is greater than at the waist. When you press down along the edge, you therefore have a stronger resistance acting at the wider contact points than at the narrower contact points. Since the widest part is at the shovel, this is where the greatest resistance is. Consequently, when you are skiing and place your ski on its edge and press down on your instep, you are creating unequal resistance along the length of the edge. Since the resistance is greatest at the shovel, the ski will pivot around that point.

Note

☐ To help visualize how this resistance works, imagine pushing a shopping trolley sideways with the brake applied to the front wheels. Rather than move sideways, the trolley will pivot around the front wheels because the resistance at the back wheels is less than at the front wheels.

Reverse camber When you press down on the middle of the ski on a compressible substance such as snow, the centre of the ski deflects more than the ends of the ski, causing the ski to bow in the reverse direction. This is referred to as reverse camber. It is the amount of reverse camber and the dimensions of the sidecut that determine the arc of a carved turn.

Reverse camber is also one of the important factors that enables a skier to initiate turns without exaggerated and exhausting body movements. When a ski is bowed in reverse camber, the ski is stressed, and stores energy. As the skier relieves the downward force on the middle of the ski by up-unweighting (springing up), the ski starts to return to its original shape and the stored energy helps 'spring' the skier into the turn in the same way as a diving board 'springs' a diver into the air or a bow releases an arrow.

Sidecut dimensions vary between ski manufacturers, but in general, giant-slalom skis have less pronounced sidecuts than slalom skis, and consequently will turn in a larger arc than slalom skis.

Torsional resistance A further feature built into skis is torsional resistance. This quality allows the ski to twist as it is turning and untwist after the turn, permitting the ski edges to maintain 'biting' contact with the snow at all times. When a skier initiates a turn, the front of the ski starts to turn and the back follows along the same path. If you immediately initiate a turn in the opposite direction, the ski's torsional resistance permits the backs of the skis to complete the last turn while the fronts of the skis twist in the new direction.

Torsional resistance varies with ski design. A beginner usually prefers a ski with less torsional resistance while a ski racer would prefer a ski with more torsional resistance.

Ski flexion Another property of modern skis is ski flexion, which determines how the ski will flex (bend) as it passes over undulations in the snow. A ski described as 'soft' will flex more than a ski described as 'stiff'. The flex pattern of a ski determines the way the ski bends in reverse camber.

The amount of flexion required in a ski depends on the type of skiing that you intend to do. For skiing on hard or icy conditions and for fast skiing it is preferable to have a reasonably stiff ski. For slower speed skiing and for skiing in powder snow most people prefer a soft ski.

While camber, sidecut, torsional resistance and flexion are the main features that determine how a ski will turn, there are a number of additional qualities built into skis that improve their overall performance at various speeds but which add to their cost. Some better quality skis have layers of rubber to help dampen ski vibrations—the shaking or chatter that occurs at high speeds. Generally, the more expensive skis are constructed with sophisticated materials, such as kevlar, and graphite, which add to their lightness and durability.

Now that you have a basic understanding of the way skis are designed to turn, you can appreciate how much easier these manoeuvres can be if you ski in such a way as to utilize these features. My experience is that those who have been skiing for many years have been taught, either by professionals or by themselves, to use exaggerated movements of their bodies in order to start the skis turning, and even though they are on modern skis they have not as yet caught on to the joys and simplicity of their modern skiing equipment. You, who are just beginning to ski, have the chance to learn to ski the·easy way, doing the minimum necessary to start the skis turning and then to control them during and after the turns. So continue on with the rest of the International Parallel Technique exercises, and not only will you ski well but you will also have lots of energy left over after a day on the slopes for the *après-ski*.

Note

□ Skis turn because of the shape of the ski, in other words, the sidecut and camber. When you traverse and put the skis on their edges (by rolling the knees) and press the ski into the snow (by pressing on the instep of the foot) the skis will turn. The more the skis are on their edge, the sharper the turn will be. Conversely, the less the skis are on edge, the larger and more gradual will be the radius of the turn. The key to making easy turns is having a good traverse position, and if you experience problems with the uphill turn manoeuvre, it is a good idea to go back and briefly practise the 'traverse-holding poles horizontal across the chest' exercise on page 38.

B   Starting on a steeper traverse

Repeat exercise A (page 57), starting on a slightly steeper traverse (track B, fig 4), and turn your skis to make a gradual stop.

C   Starting on a steep traverse

Continue to increase the steepness of the traverse tracks, in other words, tracks C and D of fig 4, each time turning your skis to make a smooth, graceful stop.

D   Turning uphill from the fall-line

Start on the fall-line (track E, fig 4 and picture sequence 35) and allow your skis to slide down the fall-line. Your weight should be carried evenly over both feet. As you pick up speed shift your weight to one ski and, treating this as nothing more than another uphill turn, steer your skis by pressing your knees as you have been doing in the previous exercises—in other words, up the hill, so that the ski with the weight on it becomes the downhill ski, and ski to a smooth stop.

Repeat exercises A–D, in the opposite direction. If an easy intermediate slope is nearby and convenient to reach, it is valuable to repeat exercises A–D on this steeper slope.

35a

35b

35d

35c

35a–d: Turning uphill from fall-line.

2 Series of 'garlands' uphill, from the fall-line

When you have mastered turning uphill from the fall-line, choose an easy intermediate slope and make a series of 'garlands' (shell patterns). To do this, start at the edge of the slope and ski down the fall-line. As soon as you start to pick up some speed, make an uphill turn and stop. Then point your skis down the fall-line again and make another uphill turn and stop. Repeat this pattern three or four times and you should end up with a track in the snow resembling a garland or shell (pictures 36a and 36b).

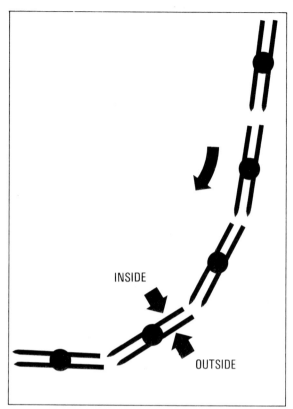

Fig 6. Outside/inside ski.

36a

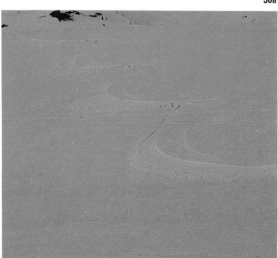

36a and 36b: Series of 'garlands' uphill.   36b

3 Crossing the fall-line using knee pressure–preparation for downhill turn

Definition of outside/inside ski

If you look at the track that skis make in the snow (fig 6), you will see that each turn inscribes an arc of a circle. There is therefore an inside to the circle and an outside to the circle. Logically, we refer to the 'outside ski' as being the ski that is on the outside of the circle and the 'inside ski' as the ski on the inside of the circle. I have found that students often find it easier to visualize which ski I am referring to when discussing certain ski manoeuvres when I refer to the skis as 'inside' or 'outside', rather than refer to them as 'uphill' or 'downhill'–which is the more common reference and which I also will employ for clarity of certain ski manoeuvres. In pictures 37a–37d, which show a pressure turn to the left, the right ski is the outside ski and the left ski is the inside ski.

4 Turn across the fall-line

To perform this manoeuvre, start in a steep traverse with your weight on both feet. (Although normally your weight should be on your downhill ski, for this exercise I would like you to start with your weight evenly distributed on both feet.) Refer to fig 7 and pictures 37a–37d. Begin traversing and put your weight over the outside ski. Press on this ski and push your knees in the direction of the turn so that the skis cross over the fall-line, and then continue to turn up the hill until you stop. Note that this is a large-radius turn performed exactly as the uphill turn, with no movement of the upper body.

Repeat the turn across the fall-line in the opposite direction.

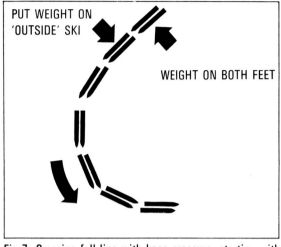

PUT WEIGHT ON 'OUTSIDE' SKI

WEIGHT ON BOTH FEET

Fig 7. Crossing fall-line with knee pressure, starting with weight on both feet.

37b

37a

37a–d: Pressure turn across fall-line to the left. 37c

37d

Tuck (egg) position.   38

5   Linking turns across the fall-line using knee pressure

When you can make a pressure turn across the fall-line on both sides, you should now try to link them up so that you can ski back and forth across the fall-line while you descend the slope. At this point in your learning process, however, linking these turns may prove too difficult, as to do so requires an ability to determine when to shift your weight from ski to ski, and a very good feel for the use of the ski edges. You may find yourself catching edges and falling as you go from one traverse position to the next. But, if you are feeling confident on your skis and found it easy to skate across the fall-line during the skating sequence, then you should try linking pressure turns across the fall-line. Remember, these are large-radius turns and are meant, at this stage of your skiing progress, to be performed on gentle beginner slopes in order that you do not pick up too much speed.

Downhill racers use pressure turns quite often while turning because these are large-radius turns and therefore do not cause them to lose much speed, and because during this manoeuvre

their skis remain in total contact with the snow, which helps them maintain good control at high speeds. Although you are not quite ready to perform these turns on the sort of slopes on which they perform, nor at the speeds they are travelling, you may enjoy imitating these racers by skiing down the gentle slopes in the tuck position, using pressure turns to cross back and forth across the fall-line. So, if time permits on this third morning and if you are feeling confident, and if the slope is not crowded, assume a tuck or 'egg' position (as shown in picture 38) and ski down the hill turning back and forth across the fall-line, making large-radius turns.

6   The tuck (egg) position

From the basic position on skis, with the skis about hip distance apart, bend forward from the waist and simultaneously crouch lower so that your weight is still over the insteps of your ski boots. You should crouch low enough so that you can rest your elbows on your knees with your ski poles pointed backwards. (Please don't point the ski poles towards the sky as I often see beginners do, as the pole tips can be very dangerous if someone should ski into them.) You will maintain better control of your skis if you keep pressing against the front of the ski boots. It is also important to keep your head up so that you can see where you are going.

Notes

□ This is a fun exercise from which to learn the subtlety of knee and ankle pressure and body lean, and to learn to feel how easy it is, and how little effort is required, to turn the skis.

□ An important principle learnt while performing the tuck position on a packed-snow slope is that as you lower your hips to crouch down, you must at the same time bend your upper body from the waist in order to keep your weight constantly over your insteps. This principle is employed during the avalement sequence in the Advanced Skiing section of this book, where you lower the hips to help absorb the moguls, and bend the upper body slightly forward from the waist to maintain control of the skis. (When skiing in deep powder snow, as explained in Section Three, you keep the upper body upright as you lower your hips, since you want your weight over your heels, rather than over your insteps.)

Whether or not you decide to try the tuck position or the pressure turns across the fall-line, you should by now be becoming well acquainted with your ski boots and skis. The boots should be feeling more comfortable and your skis should be starting to go where you want them to go. If this is so you are probably eager to get to the more difficult runs further up the mountain. However, now is the time to hold yourself in check! You have learnt how easy it is to steer your skis but you have only done an exercise that *prepares* you for the downhill turn. You must now reinforce these body movements so that they become completely second nature, since these movements are the basics of the advanced turns. The next step therefore is to build upon what you have already learnt to make a series of controlled, linked short-radius pressure turns down the slope.

Short-radius pressure turns
(basic beginner shortswing turn)

(Day 3 Afternoon)

The purpose of these exercises is:

● To learn to 'feel' the way to control the outside ski.

● To learn to make linked short-radius turns at slow speeds on gentle terrain using only knee and foot pressure.

Note

□ In order to learn the all-important value of the outside ski, and to discover how this ski controls the turn, I recommend that you ski with the skis kept approximately hip distance apart so that the inside ski does not interfere during the turn manoeuvres. Once the mastery of the outside ski has been achieved, it will be very simple to bring the skis closer together for more elegant skiing.

These exercises are to be performed on a gentle slope

1 Wide-track pressure turn across the fall-line

Start with your skis pointing off the fall-line (a steep traverse). Place your skis in a wide stance, in other words, hip distance apart, and press your shins against the fronts of the boots. Your knees should be relaxed, your shins should be leaning on the fronts of your boots, your arms held in the 'tray holding' position, and your torso naturally straight, relaxed and facing down the fall-line, as in picture 39a.

Allow your skis to slide, and maintain your wide-track position with your upper body facing down the fall-line and your weight on both feet.

Special tip

- During this entire manoeuvre, your upper body should remain relaxed, still, and always facing down the fall-line.

As you gather speed, start to turn the outside foot (and ski) in the direction of the fall-line (the left ski in pictures 39b, 39c, and 39d). To do this shift your weight on to the instep of this foot while you turn the foot.

As you can see in the sequence of pictures 39a–39e, there is no exaggerated bending at the waist or side, as is taught by some ski systems. The weight is shifted to the outside foot merely by placing the body slightly more over the outside ski, thus lightening the weight on the inside (right) ski.

As your skis cross the fall-line (pictures 39c–39e), keep your upper body still and facing down the fall-line. Maintain constant pressure on the instep of the outside foot as the skis continue to turn to the hill until the skis come to a natural stop. Repeat this turn to the opposite direction.

39a

39b

39c

39a–e: Wide-track short-radius pressure turn across fall-line.

39d

39e

Notes

□ As you turn your foot, you should also be steering with your outside knee. However, I find for this manoeuvre that it is best to think *only* about turning your foot and keeping your weight on the instep of the boot, with your shins against the fronts of the boots.

□ The object of this exercise, as previously noted, is to learn to control and steer the outside ski by applying pressure on the edge of the ski.

□ The emphasis is entirely on the outside ski during this manoeuvre. The inside ski, which is essentially weightless during the turn, will follow across the fall-line in an almost parallel manner as long as your shin is leaning against the front of the inside ski boot the entire time.

□ As you pass the fall-line (picture 39d) you can roll the inside knee (right knee in the picture) up the hill so that the skis will be parallel at the end of the turn.

□ It does not matter that the skis appear at times to be slightly angled, as the proper function of the inside ski—which results in the skis always being maintained parallel—will be learnt during the exercises of the next lesson.

2 Linked wide-track short-radius pressure turns

Once you have mastered wide-track turns to the left and right you are ready to link up these turns and make a series of turns down the hill.

Start as you did for the previous exercise and repeat the procedure. After you cross the fall-line, rather than continuing to turn your skis up the hill to stop, shift your weight to the new outside ski and turn that ski in the direction of the fall-line. After crossing the fall-line, again shift your weight to the new outside ski and turn that ski across the fall-line. Continue to make these movements all the way down the slope and you will be making a series of 'S' tracks in the snow, as in pictures 40a and 40b.

3 Pressure turns combined with skating uphill

Once you can link pressure turns, a very useful and enjoyable exercise is to make a pressure turn and then skate one step uphill.

Turn your upper body to face down the fall-line, start off on a traverse to the right and make a pressure turn to the left (body weight on your right ski). As your skis cross the fall-line, step your left ski up the hill to the left, placing the ski down on the uphill edge. Now, leaning on this uphill edge, step your right ski one step up the hill, placing it down so that the skis are running parallel, and ski to a stop. Repeat the manoeuvre in the opposite direction.

When you can perform this on both sides with good control, and at the same time feeling comfortable as you transfer your weight from ski to ski rather than stopping at the end of each manoeuvre, link a series of these combined pressure turns across the fall-line and skating uphill manoeuvres as you descend the slope.

Now you are getting close to actual skiing. You can now ski down a gentle slope making nice *controlled* linked turns. However, if you try to make these turns on a steeper slope you will start to go too fast and will undoubtedly lose control. The reason is that during these turns, the skis do not cross the fall-line quickly enough and consequently, on a steep slope, the skis pick up too much speed as they head towards the fall-line. To learn to control your skis on a steeper slope it is useful to learn the technique of down-up-down unweighting or, as the French call it, 'flexion-extension-flexion'.

40a

40a and 40b: 'S'-tracks in snow made by linked short-radius pressure turns.   40b

Parallel turns
(using flexion-extension-flexion)

(Day 4 Morning and Afternoon)

The purpose of these exercises is:

● To learn to unweight the skis with a down-up-down movement.

● To learn how to co-ordinate the pole plant with the unweighting movement.

● To link turns with down-up-down unweighting.

● To learn how to ski on moguls.

These exercises should be performed on a gentle slope

---

1 Planting ski pole using down-up-down body movement

Start in a good traverse position on a very shallow traverse. Hold the ski poles with one pole vertical and the other pointing backwards, with your arms held in the 'tray holding' position (picture 41a).

Special tip

● To bring the ski pole vertical, you merely have to cock your wrist.

Start traversing and flex your body by lowering your hips down towards the snow (your knees will automatically bend). Maintain constant shin pressure on the fronts of the ski boots and keep your upper body relaxed and facing down the fall-line. If you lock your wrist, lock your elbow and lock your shoulder, then when you lower your hips, the pole being held vertical is planted in the snow automatically (picture 41b).

From the deep 'down' position extend your hips up and forward with an exaggerated upthrust, maintaining pressure on the fronts of the ski boots (picture 41c). Try not to lift the tails off the snow. Now bring your ski pole vertical again, and then lower your hips into the flex position, plant your ski pole, and repeat the up movement. Continue to do these down-up-down movements, automatically planting the ski pole on each down movement, as you proceed across the slope.

Note

☐ I like to exaggerate the flexion-extension-flexion movements in the early learning stages until these movements are well assimilated by the body. Once your body develops a 'feel' for these movements you can stop exaggerating and start to use only as much effort as is needed to perform the manoeuvre. Eventually you will be skiing like the experts who use only the slightest movement to turn their skis.

41a

41b

41a–c (inc. overleaf): Flexion-extension-flexion unweighting with pole plant.

41c

Repeat this manoeuvre with the opposite ski pole held vertical.

Note

☐ You will probably have noticed during the last two exercises that when you made the quick up motion, the tails of your skis wanted to lift off the snow. This is because as you thrust up, you lightened the load on the ski tails. This phenomenon is called up-unweighting and we use this to help us turn our skis. By combining the steering of the skis using the knees and feet—a manoeuvre you already know—with the down-up-down motion, you can make controlled, precise parallel turns on steeper slopes.

2 Parallel turn from fall-line using flexion-extension-flexion

A Turning to the left from the fall-line
Start with your body facing down the fall-line. Your left ski pole should be vertical and your right ski pole should be pointing backwards, as in picture 42a. As you begin to pick up speed flex (lower) your hips, plant your ski pole as you did in the previous exercise and place your weight on to the right foot (which will be your outside ski during a turn to the left—picture 42b). Now, as you spring up, rather than coming up over your ski tips, dive up (similar to a dive off a divingboard), forward and around the ski pole, as in picture 42c.

Special tips

● Notice in fig 8, that the direction of your upthrust is midway between the direction your skis are pointing and the point where you plant your ski pole.

● It is important that you maintain pressure on the fronts of your ski boots, especially as you thrust upwards, and that you keep your weight on your outside (right) ski.

As you dive up and around your ski pole, your skis will automatically turn in that direction (to the left in pictures 42c and 42d). Once you have completed the up movement and your skis have crossed the fall-line you should lower your hips again and steer your skis to a stop as you have already done in the 'turn uphill' manoeuvre (pictures 42e and 42f). Keep your weight on the outside (right) ski–which now becomes your downhill ski–and your upper body in a good traverse position.

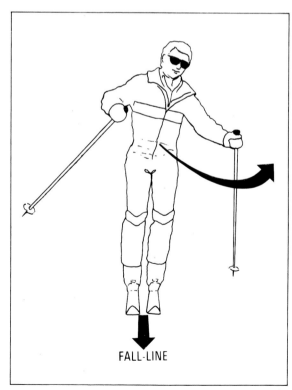

FALL-LINE

Fig 8. Direction of upthrust during parallel turn.

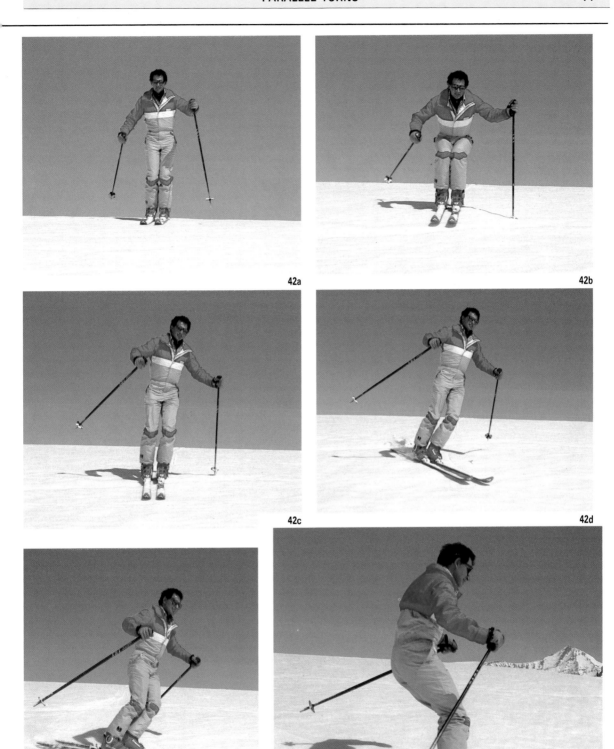

42a

42b

42c

42d

42e

42f

42a–f: Parallel turn from fall-line using exaggerated flexion-extension-flexion.

B Turning to the right from the fall-line

Repeat the previous exercise, starting with your right pole vertical, your left ski as the outside ski, and with your weight over your left foot.

3 Parallel turn across the fall-line using flexion-extension-flexion

A Steep traverse – turn to the left

Start on a steep traverse in a good traverse position with your weight on the downhill ski (the left ski in picture sequence 43) and with your downhill (left) ski pole held vertical, as in picture 43a. Start to pick up momentum, flex (lower) your hips and plant your downhill ski pole (picture 43b). As you lower your hips during the flexion movement, place your weight over both skis so that when you plant your ski pole you have the weight evenly distributed over the two skis. From this down position you are ready to dive up around the ski pole.

Just as you are ready to spring up, place your weight over the outside (right) ski and, perfor-

ming exactly the same movements that you did for the previous exercise, spring up around the ski pole (pictures 43c and 43d), allowing your skis to cross the fall-line. Then flex your hips again and steer your skis up the hill to a stop (pictures 43e and 43f) with your body in a good traverse position.

Special tip

● Should you find it difficult to perform this upwards movement, you may want to practise an exercise I employ with those of my students whose bodies seem to resist the diving motion. While traversing, crouch down in a very low position (lower your hips and upper body) and then burst up in the direction of the turn and shout 'Hallelujah' in full voice, raising your arms and entire body to the sky. As your skis turn across the fall-line (seemingly by themselves), crouch down again in the low position and, pleased that you've managed an effortless, controlled turn, say 'Glory Be', and prepare to shout 'Hallelujah' for the next downhill turn across the fall-line.

43b

43a

43c

43d

43e

B Steep traverse–turn to the right

Repeat the previous exercise, starting on a steep traverse with your right ski as your downhill ski and with your right ski pole held vertical, and perform the turn to the right.

C Shallow traverse–turn to the left

Start on a shallower traverse and perform the same parallel turn as in exercise 3A. In picture sequence 44, the parallel turn across the fall-line to the left from a shallow traverse is demonstrated, using exaggerated flexion-extension-flexion. The left pole should be in a vertical position ready to be planted and you should be in a traverse with your left ski as your downhill ski (picture 44a). With your weight on both skis, prepare to plant your ski pole (picture 44b). As in picture 44c, you should now shift your weight to your outside (right) ski and have sprung up around the ski pole. At this point you are at the maximum of your extension, with your skis starting to turn towards the fall-line and with your weight remaining on the outside (right) ski. Note in pictures 44d, 44e and 44f how the upper body remains very still. In pictures 44d and 44e the skis have crossed the fall-line and you should be lowering your hips and at the same time pressing your knees uphill (which puts the skis on their edges) while keeping pressure on the instep of your right ski boot. This causes the skis to keep carving the turn up the hill. As in picture 44f, the skis should be well edged, your body in a good traverse position and you should steer your skis uphill to a stop by maintaining the pressure on the instep of your right boot.

44a

44b

44c

43a–f: Parallel turn to the left using exaggerated flexion-extension-flexion unweighting.

43f

44d

44a–f (inc. overleaf): Parallel turn to the left
from shallow traverse using exaggerated flexion-
extension-flexion unweighting.

D   Shallow traverse–turn to the right
Repeat the previous exercise, starting on a
shallow traverse with your downhill ski being
your right ski and with your right ski pole held
vertical, and perform the turn to the right.

4   Linking large-radius parallel turns

A   Linking two turns
Start at the top of the slope in a traverse position.
Allow your skis to slide and pick up momentum.
Make a parallel turn across the fall-line as you
have done in the previous exercise, with
exaggerated down-up-down up-unweighting.
After the skis have crossed the fall-line, rather
than steer the skis to a stop, ease the pressure on
the edges and assume a neutral, relaxed posture
in the new traverse position and make another

turn across the fall-line with an exaggerated
down-up-down movement. As the skis cross the
fall-line steer them to a stop.

Special tips

● Try to make the turns large and graceful.

● Do not hurry the turn; instead, initiate the
  extension movement and allow your skis to
  turn smoothly.

B   Linking a series of large-radius parallel turns
Repeat the previous exercise. Instead of stopping
after the second turn, assume a neutral traverse
position and then turn again across the fall-line,
as in picture 45, with the same exaggerated
down-up-down movements, and continue making turns the entire way down the slope.

Special tips

● Try to maintain a good traverse position each
  time before and after the turn, with your
  weight on the downhill ski and your shins
  against the fronts of your ski boots.

● As in picture 45, you should be leaving a set of
  graceful, large-radius tracks in the snow.

Linked large-radius parallel turns.   45

Notes

☐ The most important part of the turn is the end of the turn, because it is here that you gain or lose control. Therefore, in order to link a series of smooth turns, you must be in control at the end of each one. If not, you will go into the next turn out of control and will probably shoot off wildly down the hill.

☐ The end of every turn should be the same. Whether your skis are together or apart, whether you are skiing on an easy slope or a steep slope, whether on ice, soft or hard-packed snow, you should end each turn by keeping your body in a good traverse position and steer your knees towards the hill while you lower your hips and press on the edge of the downhill ski, leaning the shins against the fronts of the ski boots.

☐ To help visualize the ending of the turn, refer to pictures 46a and 46b, which show the end of a turn with the skis apart. In picture 46a, I have finished my extension and am just beginning to steer my skis up the hill by lowering my hips and pushing my knees up the hill. You can see in picture 46b, which is taken a moment later during the end of the turn, how I control my skis by continuing to lower my hips (which puts more weight on the edge of the downhill ski) and continue to steer my skis by rolling my knees up the hill. Notice how much more my skis are on their edges.

☐ As previously mentioned, the more the skis are edged the sharper will be the turn and therefore the slower you will ski, making it easier to control your skis. Note also in pictures 46a and 46b how my body remains in a traverse position and how still my upper body remains as I complete the turn. The plume of snow that is visible in picture 46b is caused by the edge of my downhill ski pressing and carving into the snow.

5 Using moguls for turns

No ski area is free of moguls! You may find a slope from time to time without a mogul but that is quite the exception. Moguls are bumps in the snow, and although some moguls are permanent, being formed by snow piling on to a big boulder or over a large mound, most moguls are formed by skiers turning their skis in the same place, carving out the snow beneath the turn and spraying the snow to the side. This continuous carving of the snow results in a mound of snow. The steeper the slope the more turns skiers make, producing numerous moguls that are usually quite large. On a gentle slope, most skiers make fewer turns and press less hard on the edges of the skis and so the moguls tend to be smaller.

In many ski areas machines are used to flatten the moguls and redistribute the snow in order to maintain an even snow base throughout the slope; however, no sooner are the moguls flattened by the machines, than new ones are being formed by skiers.

46a

46a and 46b: End of parallel turn (with skis apart).   46b

It is therefore evident that sooner or later you will be having to manoeuvre across moguls in order to negotiate a slope. It is therefore wise to learn how to ski moguls so that instead of trying to avoid them (as I did when I first learnt to ski), you can seek them out. In fact, it is actually easier to turn your skis using a mogul than to turn your skis on a smooth, mogul-free slope.

The following exercises should be performed on an easy intermediate-grade slope with moguls

A   Turning over moguls using flexion-extension-flexion

Seek out a slope that has large round moguls. You will notice that between two moguls there is a depression, which is referred to as a trough. Troughs occur before and after every mogul.

Picture sequence 47 demonstrates how to turn over a mogul. Assume a correct traverse position and, in a shallow traverse, ski towards a mogul, as shown in picture 47a. Bring your downhill ski pole forward and begin your flexion as you enter the trough before the mogul (picture 47b). Plant your ski pole on the summit of the mogul (picture 47c). As the mogul rises up, start your extension up and in the direction of the turn (picture 47d), timing your upward movement so that you are at your full extension at the top of the mogul (picture 47e).

Special tip

● The down-up-down movement should be performed exactly as previously performed on the smooth slopes.

As your skis cross the fall-line (picture 47f), start flexing again as you enter the trough behind the mogul, and ski down the back of the mogul. Recover your ski pole by pushing your wrist forward and then, in a good traverse position, steer your skis up the hill to a stop (picture 47g).

Special tip

● You must be sure to recover your inside arm and ski pole as you pass the fall-line. Refer to pictures 47f and 47g. Skiers often have a tendency to leave this arm trailing behind as they cross the fall-line and start their flexing movement, which causes the inside shoulder to be pulled backwards so that the body is not in the correct traverse position so necessary for control at the end of the turn.

Here is a brief review of the movements for turning on a mogul: **step 1** – flex in the trough before the mogul, preparing to plant your ski pole on the summit of the mogul; **step 2** – extend your body and turn as the mogul rises up, turning over the summit of the mogul; **step 3** – flex again in the trough behind the mogul, recover your ski pole, and steer the skis to a stop.

Notes

□ Your weight should be transferred from ski to ski exactly as you did in the previous exercises on the smooth slopes.

□ In pictures 47a and 47b, my weight is on my left (downhill) ski. In picture 47c, my weight is on both feet, and in pictures 47d–47g, my weight is on my right (outside) ski, which in pictures 47f and 47g, is now my new downhill ski.

□ You will no doubt notice that if you thrust upwards with the same force that you used to turn on the smooth slopes, you will be thrown through the air as you come off the top of the mogul and will not be able to maintain your skis in contact with the snow. This is because the rise of the mogul helps give you lift and aids the up-unweighting of the skis. Since so little of the ski is in contact with the snow (in picture 47e only the area of the ski under the foot is in the snow) there is very little resistance to the skis turning. Therefore, in order to maintain the constant 'feel' for the snow, you should moderate the upthrust during the extension movement whenever turning on the top of a mogul.

◻ Once you have practised turning on a few moguls and got the timing right, you will begin to realize how easy and enjoyable it can be and will hopefully start to look for moguls for your turns.

◻ Naturally, you must practise turning over moguls on both sides.

B   Linking turns while turning over moguls

Once you feel comfortable turning to the left and to the right over the moguls you should choose a short mogul field on an easy intermediate slope and practise linking your turns. Begin by linking two turns and stopping. When you have mastered this, link together three and then four turns and finally ski through the mogul field turning over as many moguls as you can. Between each turn assume a neutral, relaxed traverse position so that you can flex your hips before the next turn.

Note

◻ Turning over the moguls is a very good way to help reinforce the parallel turn as, due to minimal resistance at the top of the mogul, the two skis turn easily. It is also a nice way to ski on gentle and intermediate turns at slow speeds. However, on steeper slopes, the moguls are often very large and if you turn on the top you may find a metre or more dip at the back of the mogul that you must drop into to complete the turn. Also, if you approach a mogul too fast on even a gentle or intermediate run, you will find it difficult to keep your skis in the snow; often you will fly off the top of the mogul, and need to turn your skis in the air, and to try and regain your balance on landing. (This, by the way, can be fun once you get the hang of it. During lessons with advanced skiers we sometimes play games by skiing down a mogul field, jumping off the tops of the moguls and trying to pass over two or three moguls while in the air before turning our skis and landing in the new direction. However, this is a form of acrobatic or trick skiing and should not be attempted until you are ready for it.)

In situations when you are skiing too fast to turn over the mogul in good control, if the mogul is too large to ski down comfortably, if the mogul is a rock, partially covered with snow, or if there is an obstacle such as a tree growing out of the mogul, it is much easier to ski around it.

C   Turning around moguls using flexion-extension-flexion

Once again, as in the previous exercise, the up-unweighting of the ski is done with a down-up-down body movement. In fact, turning around a mogul is essentially the same as turning on a smooth slope, since you will be turning on the reasonably smooth path between the moguls.

Start in a traverse position and aim for a point just above a mogul. As you approach this point bring your downhill ski pole forward to a ready position (picture 48a). Now start your flexion movement and prepare to plant your ski pole just above the mogul (picture 48b). From this position, extend up and around the ski pole and turn your skis around the mogul so that as you are extending you pass in the trough to the side of the mogul (pictures 48c and 48d). As your skis cross the fall-line again lower your hips and steer your skis to a stop up the hill (pictures 48e and 48f). Repeat on the opposite side.

Special tip

● Be sure not to let your inside arm drag behind as you cross the fall-line, but instead recover your arm and ski pole by pressing your wrist forward as you start your flexion movement, as shown in picture 48e.

Notes

◻ During this manoeuvre more of your ski will remain in contact with the snow while turning than was the case when you were turning over the mogul. This extra contact will help you maintain good control throughout the turn.

◻ To help control your speed on steep runs, try to make the turn as wide as possible so that your skis ride up the front slope of the neighbouring mogul.

47d

47c

47a–g: Turn to the left over mogul using flexion-extension-flexion.

47e

47b

47a

47f

47g

48a

48b

48c

48a–f: Parallel left turn around mogul using flexion-extension-flexion.

48d

48e

48f

D Linking turns while turning around moguls

Choose the same moguls as you did for exercise 2, and repeat the exercise, turning around the moguls, rather than over them. Start by linking two turns, then three, then four and finally ski through the mogul field, turning around as many moguls as you can. Try to control your speed so that you feel you could stop at any moment you chose. The emphasis at this point should be on style and control rather than on speed.

E Foot swivel on top of a mogul

This is an exercise which I recommend to intermediate skiers who find it difficult to keep their skis parallel while they are turning. It is also a very good exercise for increasing the sensitivity of the feet and ankles relative to the changes of pitch in terrain.

   Stand on top of a mogul with only the part of the ski that is beneath the feet in contact with the snow—in other words, the front and back parts of the ski should be in the air. Reach down the fall-line and plant your ski pole, as in picture 49a. Keep your weight on both feet and ensure that

your shins are leaning against the fronts of the ski boots. Flex your hips a little so that you are not standing up straight. Holding on to the ski pole, and with only a very slight upwards movement, swivel your feet so that your skis turn across the fall-line beneath you, ending in the new traverse position (pictures 49b, 49c and 49d).

Special tips

- Try to remain as much in one place as possible while foot swivelling around the ski pole, and try not to pick up any speed. (Many skiers, when first trying this, shoot off down the back of the mogul.)

- Be sure that the skis are close together so that they are turning at essentially the same part of the mogul.

- It is important to plant the ski pole down the fall-line so that you have to reach downhill.

- As in picture 49a, the ski pole should be kept vertical as you make the turn.

49a

49b

49c

49d

49a–d: Foot swivelling to the left on top of mogul.

Large-radius parallel turns on gentle slopes

(Day 5 Morning)

The purpose of these exercises is:

- To have fun.
- To gain more control and precision through practice.
- To reinforce the body movements required to make controlled parallel turns.
- To explore more of the mountain.
- To learn the stop turn.

You've made it! All the exercises of the previous four days are ready to be put into practice. If you have been able to perform these exercises correctly, you now have the technique and capability to ski down the gentle runs on the mountain in good control and with a graceful action.

1 Skiing down gentle runs making large-radius parallel turns

Choose a gentle (novice) run and start skiing. Concentrate on exaggerating your flexion-extension-flexion movements as you turn from one traverse to the next. Look for moguls and ski over them, and then look for more moguls and ski around them. Start off skiing slowly and, as you gain more confidence, gradually increase your speed.

Try to link large-radius parallel turns, making them smooth and graceful, and ski as many different novice runs as you can, enjoying the changing views and conditions that you encounter.

Special tip

- Be sure to concentrate on controlling your skis at the end of each turn.

2 The stop turn

Now that you are skiing some of the runs on the mountain, it may be a good idea to put aside a few minutes and practise the stop turn, which is an emergency ski manoeuvre used to bring your skis very rapidly across the fall-line to the 'perpendicular to the fall-line' position. While you are skiing, you may encounter any number of circumstances, such as a skier falling just in front of you, a rock immediately in the direction you are heading, a patch of blue ice, a bare patch, a deep depression in the snow, a chunk of hard snow left by the snowpacking machine or having fallen from a slope above, or even, in some ski areas, a cliff to one side of the run which requires you to come to a very abrupt halt. The stop turn is therefore very useful to master.

Start by facing down the fall-line and begin skiing down it in a neutral body position with your weight on both feet (picture 50a). When you are ready to stop, lower your hips and exaggerate the flexion, and plant your ski pole at your side (picture 50b). From this low position, burst up rapidly and twist your skis beneath you (picture 50c), bringing your skis towards the perpendicular to the fall-line (picture 50d).

As your skis come to the perpendicular to the fall-line, set the edges by rolling your knees sharply uphill and simultaneously lean your upper body over your skis by bending from your waist down the fall-line so that your weight is completely over the instep of your downhill ski boot, with the skis well edged, as in picture 50e.

Naturally, you should practise this on both sides, though you will probably find that doing it to one side seems more comfortable than to the other. Most skiers have a side they prefer, and although you should work on your basic turns so that they feel equally good on both sides, this stop turn is an emergency manoeuvre and therefore it is more important that you perfect this at least on your preferred side.

50a

50b

50c

50a–e: Stop turn to the left.   50d

50e

Special tip

● As a fun means of learning the stop turn, place two ski poles in the snow (as in picture 51a). Ski towards the poles and, at the last possible moment, burst up and stop, without knocking the poles over (pictures 51b and 51c).

Note

☐ There are two ways to rapidly turn your skis. One is by bursting up with rapid up-unweighting as has just been explained, and the other is by rapidly down-unweighting and twisting your skis beneath you as you quickly lower your hips. My experience is that up-unweighting is the far better way of turning your skis and maintaining control during most parallel turns, and is more useful in most snow conditions. Therefore I have emphasized the up-unweighting manoeuvre in the International Parallel Technique. Consequently, I teach the stop turn at this point in the teaching sequence using up-unweighting. As you become a more advanced skier you will learn to turn your skis in certain conditions using down-unweighting and once you have mastered down-unweighting, you can perform the stop turn with the down-unweighting movement, which actually brings the skis across the fall-line faster, as explained on page 174 of Section Three.

51a

51b

51a–c: Stop turn—stopping just before ski poles.

51c

Large-radius parallel turns on easy intermediate slopes

(Day 5 Afternoon)

The purpose of these exercises is:

- To have fun.

- To gain more control and confidence on steeper slopes.

- To reinforce the body movements required to make controlled turns on steeper slopes.

- To link parallel turns on an intermediate slope.

As explained in the Introduction, the goal of the International Parallel Technique is to be able to make controlled, linked, large-radius parallel turns on easy intermediate slopes. If, during the previous lesson, you thought that you fell too much or often felt out of control, then it would probably be worthwhile to spend another session on the gentle (novice) slopes, concentrating on controlling your skis at the end of each turn. But if you enjoyed skiing on those runs and were comfortable making controlled parallel turns, you should now be thoroughly prepared to accomplish this goal.

Skiing down easy intermediate runs making large-radius parallel turns

Choose an easy intermediate run and start skiing. As you did in the previous lesson concentrate on exaggerating the flexion-extension-flexion movements as you turn from one traverse to the next. Also concentrate on controlling your skis after the turn, as this is the most important part of the turn and the part where you will either maintain

or lose control of your skis. Start off slowly, making a series of smooth, large-radius turns as shown in picture 52. Stop every so often and check your tracks to see that they are round and smooth.

As you gain confidence you can increase your speed and begin to moderate the amount of down-up-down movement you use for the turns. Seek out moguls and turn over them when you are skiing slowly and turn around them when you are skiing faster. Ski different intermediate runs, gradually increasing the steepness of the runs you choose and enjoy the variations in the terrain and locale. Towards the end of the afternoon you should be skiing with little effort and plenty of style and control.

You should now be a parallel skier, capable of happily skiing many of the intermediate runs on the mountain.

Tracks showing smooth, linked, large-radius parallel turns. **52**

What next?

Continue to practise and perfect the large-radius parallel turns on various intermediate runs. When you feel that you would like to tackle the steeper, more difficult slopes, you should learn what I call the basic advanced-skier shortswing turn, which follows in Section Two. This turn will enable you to ski the advanced intermediate slopes with the same control and confidence as you have on the easy intermediate slopes. Once you have mastered this shortswing turn, it will only be a matter of learning to apply this manoeuvre to varying steepnesses and snow conditions to put you in the category of advanced skier.

Advanced Skiing

In the introduction to Section One, I mentioned that most of the exercises of the International Parallel Technique are actual ski movements used in advanced skiing. If you have performed the exercises in Section One then you are fully prepared now to become an advanced skier, as you have learnt how to ski with the lower body while using the upper body for balance. In the advanced skiing position the upper part of the body is always facing down the fall-line and remains relatively still while the work of turning and steering the skis is done by the feet, ankles and knees. The hips are used to help unweight the skis, and the torso is used as a counter-balance to keep the weight properly over the skis.

As an intermediate skier you are capable of making large-radius parallel turns. But in order to control your speed on steeper slopes it is necessary to be able to make short-radius turns (with unweighting), since the short-radius turns prevent the skis from picking up as much speed as is attained during the execution of large-radius turns.

To learn the short-radius turn with up-unweighting (or shortswing turn, as it is also called) I have developed a teaching sequence that I call the Tea-for-two Ski Dance. This manoeuvre places the student in the advanced skiing position and, through a series of exercises, teaches the shortswing turn, which can then be used to ski through mogul fields, on steep slopes, on ice, off-piste (off-trail), on varied snow conditions and—with a slight modification of body position—in deep powder snow. This then, once mastered, is the basic position for all skiing. The end result of this sequence of exercises incorporates all the techniques taught in the previous nine lessons of the International Parallel

Technique, and automatically has the skier skiing with 'anticipation' (an advanced man-oeuvre developed by ski racers).

I call this teaching sequence the Tea-for-two Ski Dance because I ask my students to sing the song 'Tea-for-two' while descending the slope during the lessons (with the younger skiers I use some other song that they may know, with a suitable rhythm, such as a slow version of 'Twinkle, Twinkle, Little Star'. The reason that I ask my students to sing these songs is to emphasize the rhythm of the shortswing turn. In fact, having completed the nine lessons of Section One, you already have the required technique to make shortswing turns, for once you can make correct large-radius turns using flexion-extension-flexion, all that is necessary is to learn the rhythm for the shortswing turn with the body in the correct position on the skis.

The key to making smooth short-radius turns is to *allow* the skis to turn, not to force them. As noted in Section One, modern skis are designed to turn, and therefore the object of the Tea-for-two Ski Dance is to combine rhythm with proper body movement to enable the skis to turn as they were designed to do. I often like to draw an analogy with horseback riding, where all you have to do to make the horse turn left or right is sit properly in the saddle, pull on the reins and apply some leg pressure to the horse's flanks. It is not necessary nor recommended to thrust yourself about in order to coax the horse to turn. In skiing, you have to stand astride the skis properly and similarly 'pressure' the ski by pressing on the ski edges in a specific manner. Then the skis will turn. The down-up-down unweighting helps the skis turn more easily and in a short radius.

Shortswing turns

(the 'Tea-for-two' ski dance)

The same successful learning formula used for the International Parallel Technique is applied to the learning sequence for the shortswing turn. The basic body movements of the shortswing are first practised on very easy slopes without speed, in order to learn the rhythm and weight shifting without having to worry about skiing out of control. Once these are understood, the short-swing is performed on increasingly steeper slopes at increasingly higher speeds.

At first the shortswing is done with the skis kept very wide apart and with exaggerated flexion-extension-flexion unweighting move-ments, and then as you become more at ease with the manoeuvre, the skis are brought together and the amount of flexion-extension-flexion is sub-stantially reduced.

After practising the seven interlocking exer-cises in order, you should be able to ski graceful, controlled shortswing turns on advanced in-termediate slopes. Exercise 8, on page 97, explains how to combine the shortswing rhythm and large-radius turns to ski very narrow, crowded runs.

This exercise should be performed on flat terrain

---

1 Learning the shortswing rhythm and weight shifting (without speed)

Use picture sequence 53 as a guide. Stand with your skis approximately hip distance apart. Your upper body should be upright and relaxed, your head centred, your arms in the 'tray holding' position and the ski poles held vertical, with the tips just out of the snow. Lean your shins against the fronts of the ski boots for support, and relax your knees.

Now roll both knees towards each other so that you are standing on the inner edges of both skis. (During this entire exercise you should keep both knees rolled inwards towards each other.) Lower your hips and lean all your weight over one ski (picture 53a). Since your knee is rolled inwards, your weight will be over the inner edge of this ski. From this position, fully extend upwards (picture 53b) and then again lowering your hips, reposition your upper body so that your weight will come down over the inner edge of the other ski (right ski in picture 53c).

Special tips

● Try to keep your torso straight without bending from the waist.

● Be sure that you don't 'swing' your hips from side to side as you would do in a 'twist' dance, but instead move your hips and torso up as a unit, over to the side, and down.

Repeat this motion, as shown in pictures 53d, 53e and 53f, so that you now push up off the inner edge of the right ski and your hips and torso move up, over, and down again on the inner edge of the left ski. Continue to repeat this motion a number of times.

Once you can feel that you are doing it correctly you can sing or hum 'Tea-for-two' and co-ordinate the down and up movements with the down and up beats of the song so that the down movements take longer and the up movement is more rapid. Co-ordinating with the words of the song, 'Tea' is the down movement; 'For' is the rapid up movement; 'Two' is the down movement (with the weight transferring to the opposite ski); 'And' is the rapid up movement; 'Two' is the down movement (with the weight transferring to the opposite ski); 'For' is the rapid up movement; and 'Tea' is the down movement, with the weight again transferring to the opposite ski.

Since you are holding the ski poles vertically, if you keep your shoulder, elbow and wrist locked as you lower your hip over the inner edge of the

53a

53b

53c

53d

53e

53f

53a–f: Learning rhythm and weight shifting for shortswing turn on the flat.

ski, the corresponding ski pole will automatically be planted in the snow, as in pictures 53a, 53c and 53f.

Now that you can do this on the flat you should have no trouble performing this while gliding on a gentle slope.

These exercises should be performed on a gentle slope

2 Learning the shortswing rhythm and weight shifting while schussing the fall-line

Start by facing down the fall-line with your skis approximately hip distance apart and your body as it was in the previous exercise. Push off with your ski poles, and then hold them in the 'tray holding' position, but pointed vertically downwards as you gain momentum.

Keep your knees rolled towards each other and, while gliding slowly, perform exactly the same movements as you did while standing still in the previous exercise, singing or humming 'Tea-for-two' and co-ordinating the up and down movements with the up and down beats of the song.

Special tips

● As you shift your weight from side to side your skis may have a tendency to turn off the fall-line. For this exercise you should try to maintain your skis pointing straight down the fall-line while you do the down-up-down weight shifting movements.

● Since you do not want to gain much speed, choose a section of the gentle slope that is just steep enough to allow the skis to glide and one that runs down the fall-line.

3 Wide-track shortswing turn using exaggerated flexion-extension-flexion

Once you can correctly co-ordinate the rhythm and the down-up-down movements so that your weight comes down on the inner edge of the ski, you are ready to start to turn your skis across the fall-line. At this early stage of learning the

shortswing turn do not be concerned about how expert you look; in fact, I often refer to this as 'sloppy shortswing'. The emphasis is to be on rhythm and learning to shift your weight from inner edge to inner edge, with up-unweighting while the skis turn from side to side. I therefore strongly recommend that you keep your skis quite wide apart and that you exaggerate the down-up-down movements, as this will help to accomplish that goal.

Start with your skis on a steep traverse and push off with your ski poles to gain speed. Hold your poles ready to be planted. As you are gliding, lower your hips so that your weight is over the inside edge of your downhill ski (the left

54a   54b

54h

foot in picture 54a). As you reach the lowest point of the flexion movement your ski pole will automatically be planted in the snow (picture 54b) and you should begin to push up off that edge as you start your extension movement (picture 54c). Keep your upper body facing down the fall-line and concentrate only on thinking about the 'Tea-for-two' rhythm and transferring your weight to the opposite inner edge while you lower your hip during the following flexion (pictures 54d and 54e) as you did in the previous exercises. The skis will turn seemingly of their own accord, the important point being that you do not have to force your skis around. As you reach the lowest point of the flexion, push up again off the ski edge and, transferring your weight, allow your skis to turn across the fall-line. Continue singing 'Tea-for-two' as you shortswing down the run.

In picture 54e my weight is coming down on the inside edge of my right ski, I am about to plant my right ski pole and extend up. In picture 54f, I extend up and allow my skis to turn right, with the weight coming down on the inner edge of my left ski (picture 54g).

When you want to stop, instead of making another extension continue lowering your hips and pressing down on the inner edge of the ski and your skis will continue turning uphill, coming to a smooth stop (picture 54h).

54c   54d   54e

54g   54f

54a–h: Shortswing turns to left and right using exaggerated down-up-down unweighting.

Notes

□ It is best not to intellectualize the act of turning the skis, as it can be very confusing while skiing to think about all the movements necessary to turn your skis. The Tea-for-two Ski Dance is an approach to learn to make shortswing turns using rhythm and weight shifting, but the actual turning of the skis is performed exactly as you have already done when making large-radius turns. Therefore, having made large-radius turns your body knows what it must do to turn the skis.

□ A series of shortswing turns is nothing more than a series of large-radius turns with the traverse (the neutral body position) eliminated between turns. During large-radius turns there is a separate ending to each turn and a separate start to the next turn. In a short-radius turn the end of one turn *is* the beginning of the next turn.

In figs 9a and 9b, you can see that the actual turn across the fall-line is the same for both shortswing and large-radius turns. The only difference is that when making the shortswing turns you eliminate the traverse between the turns and hook the turns together.

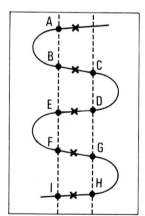 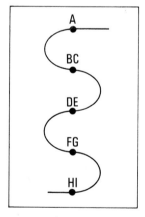

Fig 9a. Large-radius turns.   Fig 9b. Shortswing turns.

4   Wide-track shortswing practice on a gentle slope

Having learnt to perform the shortswing manoeuvre during the previous exercise, it is a good idea to practise making shortswing turns down a smooth, easy slope so that the movements start to feel natural and comfortable. Still keeping your skis about hip distance apart, continue on the first few runs to exaggerate the down-up-down unweighting, as not only will this exaggeration help you to perform the shortswing turn, but also knowing how to exaggerate will be very useful when you start to ski in deep powder. After a few runs, you can begin to moderate the down-up-down movements and gradually bring your skis closer together.

5   Shortswing turns with weight on both feet

When the skis are kept a distance apart, a good skier has the option of skiing with his or her weight on one ski at a time, or on both skis. But whenever the skis are brought very close together it is best to ski with your weight distributed evenly on both feet and to think of the two skis as a single wide ski with a joint in the middle. This is because when your skis are together, in order to keep all your weight on the inside edge of the downhill ski, it is necessary to assume an extremely angled body position ('comma' position) as in picture 55a, leaning your torso out over the downhill ski while your knees are rolled uphill. Although this was the way I was taught to ski years ago and is very stylish, I have since found out how much easier and more comfortable it is to ski with the upper body in a more upright and relaxed position. Having your weight on both feet when your skis are close together allows you to keep your upper body in this upright relaxed position (picture 55b). The following exercises lead to making shortswing turns with your weight on both feet.

A   Starting the turn with separated skis and finishing with skis together

Begin as you did in exercise 3 on page 90. Perform your flexion and extension with your feet wide apart, as shown in pictures 56a and 56b. After your skis have crossed the fall-line and you are starting your next flexion movement, bring your top ski alongside the downhill ski (picture 56c) and continue your flexion movement with your

Body position with weight all on downhill ski
(skis together).   55a

Body position with weight on both skis
(skis together).   55b

56b

56a

56c

56d

56a–d: Shortswing turning with separated skis, ending with the skis together and weight on both skis.

57a

weight coming down over both skis (picture 56d) and then, pressing down on both feet, continue turning your skis until they stop. Repeat this movement on the opposite side.

B Linking turns with the skis close together

Repeat the previous exercise, but instead of stopping when your skis cross the fall-line and your weight is on both skis, push up off the edges of both skis and make the next shortswing turn (pictures 57a–57e). Keep your skis close together and your weight over both skis and, flexing and extending, make a series of three or four shortswing turns.

57b

57c

57e

57d

57a–e: Linking shortswing turns with skis close together and weight on both feet.

C Practice shortswing turns with the skis close together

On the same gentle slope used for exercise 4, start skiing with your skis apart and your weight over one ski using exaggerated flexion and extension movement. As you are completing the first turn, bring your skis together and place your weight over both feet and continue skiing down the slope with your skis held close together and your weight over both skis, making a series of linked shortswing turns. As these turns start to feel comfortable, gradually reduce the amount of flexion and extension until you are skiing with only a trace of down-up-down movements.

Note

☐ Once you feel comfortable with the shortswing turns on gentle slopes and can ski equally well with your weight on one ski at a time or on both skis, you are ready to apply this turn to more difficult slopes and conditions. The basic movement will always remain the same. On steeper slopes, on mogulled slopes and on ice, more precise control of the edges will be required. On ice and on steeper slopes, controlling the downhill ski is very important and you will probably want to ski with more of your weight on the downhill ski, while on easy slopes and in powder snow it is preferable to ski with your weight evenly over both feet.

6 Shortswing turns on easy intermediate slopes with moguls

The best way to ski shortswing turns on a mogulled slope is to turn around the moguls rather than turning on their tops.

On an easy intermediate slope choose a ski path that runs straight down the fall-line through the moguls. Start off building a good rhythm by linking a series of shortswing turns on the smooth section of the slope above the moguls, and then ski through the mogul field maintaining the same rhythm, planting your poles on the front flank of the mogul near the summit and turning your skis in the troughs between the moguls (as shown in pictures 58a–58d).

58a

58b

58c

58d

58a–d: Linking shortswing turns through mogul field.

7 Shortswing turns on advanced intermediate slopes

An important point to remember while making shortswing turns is that you must always face your upper body down the fall-line. This is very important when skiing on steeper slopes. It is also a good idea to exaggerate the down movement of the down-up-down unweighting in order to control your speed, by turning the skis further from the fall-line as you complete each turn. Furthermore, when first practising skiing on an advanced intermediate slope, you should ski as slowly as you can, concentrating on maintaining good control of your skis at all times.

I recommend that on these and steeper slopes you ski with your skis kept about 7.5–12.5 cm (3–5 in) apart (as shown in picture sequence 59) and that you shift your weight from ski to ski rather than skiing with your weight evenly distributed over both skis.

Choose a smooth advanced intermediate slope and practise making a series of linked shortswing turns. As recommended above, exaggerate your down movements and transfer your weight from ski to ski. When you feel confident making these turns, seek out some moguls on these advanced intermediate slopes and shortswing through the moguls.

59a

59b

59c

59d

59a–d: Shortswing turns on advanced intermediate slopes.

8 Skiing on very narrow ski runs

Many ski areas have ski runs that are in fact snow-covered roads and consequently very narrow. In the European ski areas these types of runs often have a wall of earth or rock on one side and a drop-off on the other (as can be seen in picture 60). As these ski runs are usually the way back to town or to the ski area and are not steep, all grades of skiers can be found on them at the end of the day. Beginners generally snowplough down the middle of the run and the experts schuss or 'wedel' (make quick shortswing turns) along the edge. Intermediate skiers, not being as surefooted as the experts, usually get caught up behind the beginners. However, once you can ski the shortswing turn, you can combine this with large-radius turns and swing your way down the narrow run, making turns around the beginners.

It is useful to imagine a line running down the centre of the narrow run, and to call this the 'pole-planting line'. Each time you approach this line you should flex (lower) your hips and plant your ski pole on the line.

To learn to ski on a narrow ski run, choose one that isn't crowded. Start in a traverse position with your body facing down the run, as in picture 61a, and traverse across the ski run. As you approach the imaginary line running down the centre of the run, lower your hips and start to plant your ski pole on the 'line' (picture 61b). Extend up and around your ski pole (picture 61c) and swing a large-radius turn, keeping your upper body facing down the run in the basic advanced skiing position (page 87). Now complete the large-radius turn (picture 61d) and again begin to flex for the next turn as you approach the centre of the ski run (picture 61e).

Notes

☐ This turn is essentially a large-radius turn using the shortswing body position and rhythm.

☐ When there are snowploughers in the middle of the ski run, you must time the speed, acceleration and arc of your turns so that you turn safely around these skiers leaving plenty of space between you and them.

☐ When the narrow ski runs are not crowded, and especially if the sides are banked, it is great fun to make your turns using the full width of the ski run, so that your skis swing from one side of the run to the other while your upper body tends to remain close to the centre line.

Narrow ski run returning to bottom of mountain.

60

61a–e: Skiing on a very narrow ski run with imaginary line running down the centre.

Anticipation

'Anticipation' was developed by ski racers to make the initiation of the turn easier. All skiers should incorporate anticipation in their skiing repertoire and, as previously pointed out, if you are skiing in the basic advanced skiing position, as described on page 87, then when you are making shortswing turns you are automatically using anticipation to help start your turns. I always ski shortswing with anticipation and I use 'extreme anticipation' when I am skiing the very steep slopes and gullies.

To ski with anticipation you must anticipate the turn with your upper body. To do this you must plant your ski poles further back, and further down, the fall-line than you would normally do for the basic large-radius turn.

When I was taught to ski we used longer ski poles and the poles were planted by the shovel of the downhill ski. We then jumped our skis across the fall-line using the pole plant and the fronts of the skis as a pivot. Nowadays we use shorter ski poles and if you were to plant the ski pole at the ski shovel, your downhill shoulder would have to be brought forward, resulting in an incorrect traverse position.

In order to maintain a proper traverse position as you prepare for large-radius turns, you should plant your ski pole at your side, slightly forward of the front of your ski boots. To ski with anticipation you must plant your ski pole further back than that. Exactly where you plant your ski pole depends on the slope's steepness and your degree of anticipation. In pictures 62a–62d, I demonstrate variations in anticipation.

Picture 62a shows a pole plant with *no* anticipation. Picture 62b shows the anticipation that would be used on an advanced intermediate slope: the ski pole is planted down the fall-line on a line from the back of the ski boot. Picture 62c shows the anticipation that would be used on an expert slope: the ski pole is planted down the fall-line, approximately one-third of a metre (about a foot) behind the ski boot. Picture 62d shows the anticipation used when skiing in steep, narrow gullies to help initiate the turn with very little speed: the ski pole is planted down the fall-line below the tail of the ski.

Pole plant with no anticipation. 62a

Anticipation on advanced intermediate slopes. 62b

Anticipation on expert slopes. 62c

Extreme anticipation in steep gullies. 62d

63a

63b

To learn to ski with anticipation, choose a traverse track on any slope and prepare to make a large-radius turn. (Sequence 63 shows a turn to the left on an advanced intermediate run.) As you begin your flexion, turn your body in the direction of the turn (as shown in picture 63b) and, keeping your shoulder, elbow and wrist fixed, plant your ski pole as you lower your hips. Because you turned your upper body in the direction of the turn, you will automatically be planting your ski pole further back than you have done previously when making large-radius turns. Release the turn by extending up and around the pole (picture 63c), and you will find that your skis turn with less effort than the same turn without the anticipation. Finish the turn in the usual manner, in other words, in a good traverse position, steering the skis with your knees and ankles (pictures 63d and 63e).

Practise making turns to both sides using anticipation, and then link a series of large-radius turns, anticipating the start of each turn.

Note

☐ The easiest way to ski with anticipation is to ski shortswing turns and continually face down the fall-line with a still, relaxed upper body and with your hands held in the 'tray holding' position as your skis swing from side to side. Then, as you lower your hips, you will automatically be planting your ski pole in the correct place.

63c

63a–e: Turning with anticipation.   63d   63e

Banking the turns

I am basically a lazy skier and I like to take as much advantage as possible of natural forces to help me turn my skis. Since gravity is always acting on us to pull us down the hill I try to use this power to help initiate the turn. I also like to take advantage of momentum and the centrifugal forces that act on the body as the skis sweep through a turn at high speeds to allow me to ride up the banks of runs and up the sides of moguls during the turn. In addition to being good fun, riding up the banks and sides of moguls is an excellent way to slow down while turning, without causing you to alter your skiing rhythm.

1 Using gravity to help initiate a turn

On a steep slope, if you offset your upper body as you perform the down motion at the start of the turn by leaning it down the fall-line as you plant your ski pole, then the force of gravity will try to pull you over. (Your pole plant and your ski edges digging into the snow prevent you from falling or sideslipping.) If you now release the turn with a slight extension and rolling of the knees and ankles in the direction of the turn, you will find that your skis will turn very easily. You will in effect be using the pull of gravity rather than your leg power to start the ski tips turning.

In pictures 64a and 64b I demonstrate on a steep slope the different places where you should plant the ski pole in order to use gravity to help start the turn. In picture 64a I plant my ski pole at my side, which will require me to do a full extension of my lower body in order to turn my skis. In picture 64b, I reach further down the fall-line, offsetting my upper body, which will allow me to use gravity to help start my skis turning.

Notes

□ Using gravity to help start the ski tips turning can be done on any steep pitch or abrupt change in terrain. We also employ the pull of gravity when 'foot swivelling on top of a mogul' (exercise 5E, page 81) to help start the skis swivelling.

□ By combining extreme anticipation and banking, you can make a very slow controlled turn on a steep pitch from even a standstill with essentially no effort of your lower body. (This is further elaborated in the section on 'steep gully skiing' on page 141.)

Normal ski pole planting at side on steep slope.   64a

'Offsetting' upper body by planting ski pole further down fall-line on steep slope.   64b

65b

65a

65c

65d

65a–e: Banking turns around mogul.   65e

2 Banking on uphill slopes during a turn

A Banking around moguls

As you ski through a mogul field at speed, it is best to turn around the moguls (as explained in exercise 5C, page 77). However, as you rhythmically turn in the troughs between the moguls you will be maintaining a constant speed. Should you decide that you would like to ski more slowly and still maintain the same rhythm, you can do so by steering your skis up the sides of the neighbouring moguls as the skis turn across the fall-line, resulting in a banked turn. The further up the mogul you steer your skis, the more your skis will slow down.

Picture sequence 65 shows how to bank turns through a mogul field. In picture 65b the banked turn to the left is initiated by leaning your upper body down the fall-line as you plant your ski pole. As you perform the extension, steer your skis on a very large radius, so that they are turning on the up-slope of the neighbouring mogul (pictures 65c and 65d). As you slow down, continue to steer the skis through the turn and complete it in the normal manner (picture 65e) in a good traverse position.

You should practise banking turns on both sides and then link three or four turns together. Once you have mastered banking turns around moguls, you can ski these turns through the mogul fields.

B Airplane turns on ravine walls

When you are on a ski run that travels down a ravine with walls (steep banks) on both sides, it is exhilarating to ski up and down these walls making airplane turns. To perform banked airplane turns you must build up a fair amount of speed and then ski up one of the sides of the ravine (as shown in picture 66a). Prior to running out of speed, bank your turn by leaning your body towards the centre of the ravine as you plant your ski pole (picture 66b), extend up and around the ski pole (picture 66c) and, holding your arms out like the wings of an airplane, steer your skis across the fall-line, turning them on the side of the wall (pictures 66d and 66e). Even though your body leans towards the horizontal, centrifugal force will prevent you from falling.

As your skis cross the fall-line, continue to press your shins against the fronts of the ski boots and accelerate down the side of the ravine, shoot across the middle of the slope and ski up the other side of the ravine, repeating the same banking movements.

Notes

☐ Obviously this manoeuvre should not be performed on crowded ski runs. Be very alert to the presence of other skiers when shooting across the middle of the run.

☐ Some people may experience a loss of equilibrium and become dizzy from banking turns on very steep walls.

66a–e: Airplane turns on ravine walls.

The counter-turn
('S' turn)

On a steep slope or on a slope with moguls, a very useful manoeuvre for controlling your speed without losing your smooth rhythm is the counter-turn ('S'-turn)–the French call it the *Contre-Virage* or *Virage GT*. In this movement you use your knees and ankles to steer your skis up the hill just prior to executing a downhill turn. By turning your skis up the hill, you slow them down. Since the skis are continually turning on their edges, this is a smooth way of controlling your speed without resorting to hard edge-set checks or sideslipping. Also, by twisting and untwisting your skis you use the torsional resistance of the ski to aid the turn.

On a mogul field you can control your speed by doing counter-turns around the moguls, losing your speed on the plateau before the mogul and turning in the trough around the mogul. Though this is called a counter-turn, since the skis turn uphill away from the turn just before executing the downhill turn, it is really nothing more than an uphill turn (page 57) combined with anticipation.

67a

67b

67c

67d

1 Demonstration of a counter-turn

Before practising the exercises that teach the counter-turn, it would probably be useful to study picture sequence 67 which shows me performing a counter-turn prior to making a downhill turn to the right.

In picture 67a, I am completing a turn to the left and am flexing (lowering) my hips and pressing my knees uphill. In order to slow my skis down and still maintain my rhythm, I continue to lower my hips, press the ski edges into the snow and drive my knees uphill, bringing my ski pole vertical so that I am ready to plant it at the lowest point of my hip flexion (picture 67b). The effect of these lower body actions causes the fronts of my skis to turn further up the hill (the counter-turn) which slows the skis down. Note that the snow spray is caused by the ski edges biting into it; and there is no sideslipping.

From this controlled low position I extend up around my downhill ski pole (anticipation position)–picture 67c–and, as my skis cross the fall-line, I steer them up the hill to the right (pictures 67d, 67e and 67f) preparing for another counter-turn.

Special tips

● When you are driving your skis up the hill, as in picture 67b, it is very important to keep your upper body facing downhill so that your outside hip (right hip in picture) does not swing too far around in the direction of the turn, in order to prevent the backs of the skis from sliding away. (In this manoeuvre the backs of the skis should follow the fronts of the skis up the hill–not sideslip down the hill.)

● As you lower your hips at the end of the turn, be sure to keep your weight over the instep of your downhill ski boot (or over the middle of both boots if you have your weight on both feet).

● Try to time the pole plant so that you are planting your ski pole as you reach the lowest point of your flexion movement.

● Be sure to roll your ankles and drive your knees towards the hill as you end the turn, so that the skis are well edged and can carve into the snow rather than slip around as they turn.

● You can see in picture 67f that the track left in the snow by the counter-turn resembles an 'S'.

Since the 'downhill turn' part of this manoeuvre is essentially the same as the downhill turns you have been making during the previous ski manoeuvres, it is advisable to start off practising the 'counter' part of the counter-turn and then, when this feels comfortable, practise combining the two parts.

67e

67a–f: Counter-turn on smooth slope.

67f

68a

68b

68c

68a–d: Learning 'counter' movement of counter-turn.   68d

2   Learning the 'counter' movement of the counter-turn

Choose a moderate pitch on an easy intermediate slope and perform the manoeuvre as shown in picture sequence 68. (In this sequence the weight is on both skis.)

Start by traversing (picture 68a) and then begin to lower your hips with the weight over the middle of both ski boots and drive the fronts of your skis up the hill by steering with your knees (picture 68b). Continue flexing (lowering) your hips and steering your skis up the hill (picture 68c). Bring your downhill ski pole forward and plant it as you reach the lowest point of your flexion (picture 68d) and then stop, making sure that your skis do not sideslide down the hill. Note how, in picture sequence 68, the upper body remains still and facing down the fall-line. This prevents the outside hip from overswinging and therefore keeps the backs of the skis carving in the snow. Practise this movement on both sides.

3   The counter-turn on smooth slopes

When you feel confident performing the counter-turn uphill on both sides with a well co-ordinated pole plant, you should practise making the downhill turn from the 'counter' movement, as in picture sequence 67a–67f.

Practise at first on easy intermediate slopes and when you feel comfortable making smooth, controlled counter-turns, perform this manoeuvre on advanced intermediate slopes.

4   Practice on a mogul

When you feel confident making counter-turns on smooth slopes practise them on a mogul field on an easy intermediate slope.

Choose a small mogul and ski towards it, as shown in picture 69a. As you approach the mogul start to drive your skis up the hill on the plateau just before the mogul in a counter movement (picture 69b). As you reach the lowest part of your flexion, plant your ski pole on the top of the mogul (picture 69c), and then extend up

69c

69b

69a

69d

69e

69a–f: Counter-turns around mogul.

69f

and around your ski pole (picture 69d). Turn in the trough around the mogul (picture 69e), finishing your turn in a good traverse position (picture 69f), and aim for the next mogul.

5 Practice on steeper slopes with moguls

After making a series of slow-speed counter-turns around moguls on the easy intermediate slopes, you should practise these same turns on an advanced intermediate slope, turning around larger moguls.

Ice and hard snow conditions

I grew up skiing in the northeastern USA ski areas and therefore had to learn to ski on ice with good control. In fact, northeastern skiers can handle icy ski runs with the same ease and confidence that western USA and European skiers have on soft snow slopes. Therefore it is evident that skiing on ice is not so much a question of difficulty as it is a question of training and familiarity.

Almost all skiers will encounter icy snow conditions at some point. The snow which falls on ski areas that are at low altitudes is normally very moist, and this snow easily turns to ice when the temperature drops below freezing. Man-made snow is also often moist and becomes icy quickly. In the springtime, even high-altitude slopes that catch the hot afternoon sun thaw and then freeze during the cold nights. These western or southwestern facing slopes (northwestern, in the southern hemisphere) are usually still frozen the next morning. Should it rain, followed by the temperature dropping below freezing, the entire mountain may be covered by sheets of ice. Often, following the violent windstorms that occasionally blast the very high-altitude ski slopes, all the loose surface snow is blown off the exposed slopes leaving extremely hard or icy surfaces – this can also occur after violent major snowstorms.

In order to ski on icy slopes you must have sharp ski edges or you will find your skis slipping out from under you when you try to bite your edges into the icy snow. You also must modify your body position in order to grip the ice.

Picture 70a demonstrates a normal 'piste' traverse position. Picture 70b demonstrates a modified traverse position that should be used for skiing icy slopes. Note how much more the knees are angled in picture 70b than in picture 70a. To assume this position, roll your knees and ankles uphill, lower your hips and lean your upper body down the fall-line (bending from the waist) in order to keep most of your weight over the edge of your downhill ski. I have found that it also helps to lean your upper body slightly forward so that your weight is more over the ball of your downhill foot rather than over the instep.

Special tips

● A common fault of skiers trying to ski on ice is to 'over edge' their skis, in other words, to roll their knees and ankles too far uphill. This creates too sharp an edge angle and will usually result in the skis losing their grip and slipping out from under the skier.

● The best body position for controlling your skis on ice depends on the type of skis that you have (different model skis have different sidecuts, widths and cambers), the length of your skis, and your height and body weight distribution. It is therefore worthwhile to practise traversing and turning on an easy icy slope, angling your lower body and leaning your upper body in various ways so that you are pressing down on different places along the ski edge until you find the body position which gives you the best grip on the ice.

● For better stability on the ice it helps to separate the skis a little, though not too far apart or else it will be difficult to keep your weight over your downhill ski without having to resort to using too much angling and upper body lean. I have found a space of 5–12.5 cm (2–5 in) about right on average, though this of course can vary with the individual.

The basic motion for skiing on ice or frozen granular snow is the shortswing turn. The modifications required to ski in control on the ice are: 1 – Have your weight distributed mostly over the ball of your downhill foot (in order to control the downhill ski); 2 – Eliminate any exaggerated body movements while skiing so that you do not lose the tenuous contact between the ski edges and the icy snow; 3 – Push from ski edge to ski edge using smooth, *rapid* movements so that the ski edge bites into the snow *very briefly*. (If you try to hold the edge too long, the ski will tend to slip away.) It takes some practice to become proficient skiing on icy snow but it is definitely worthwhile putting in the time to learn, so that when you do encounter an icy ski slope you will be able to ski it confidently.

Picture sequence 70c–70f demonstrates a turn at speed on a hard surface, the angling of the lower body being very evident. Notice how still the upper body remains throughout the turn, and how it is constantly leaning forward to keep the weight over the edge of the downhill (carving) ski.

Practice shortswing turns on icy slopes

Practise making shortswing turns on an icy, gentle slope. Be sure to modify your shortswing movements as recommended previously. When you feel confident on this easy slope move on to an icy, intermediate slope.

Special tips

● Although you should not exaggerate your body movements, you must ski 'aggressively' by constantly leaning forward and over the downhill ski. People who ski ice timidly tend to lean backwards, and as soon as they do they lose control of their downhill ski, their skis go shooting off, resulting in a hard fall on the ice they were trying to avoid.

● If the icy area is just a small patch or short section of the ski run and you can see that the snow just beyond is softer, to avoid having to turn on the ice, ski across the icy section keeping the skis a comfortable distance apart and almost flat on the surface, maintaining your balance over both skis, and then make a turn in the softer snow after the icy patch.

● When coming to a stop on ice, don't try to stop sharply by digging your ski edges into the icy snow. Instead, allow yourself enough room, initiate the stop and then sideslide to a gradual stop, applying gentle pressure to the ski edges.

● Once you are capable of skiing fast and competently on ice, when you come upon a long icy section of a slope an *easy* way to negotiate this section is to make turns with

your skis kept almost flat–in other words, using very little edging–and separated so that you have good balance. With your skis almost flat you will not be able to slow yourself down much, but you can still maintain enough control through your turns to steer yourself to the softer snow beyond the icy section. There you can use your edges to slow down.

Normal 'piste' traverse position. 70a

Traverse position for 'icy' slopes. 70b

70c

70d

70e

70f

70c–f: Turn on hard snow showing lower body angling.

Avalement

Avaler, in French, means 'to swallow'. Avalement is a ski technique of swallowing the moguls. But don't worry, you do not actually have to digest the snow! What the French really mean by swallowing the moguls is absorbing them with your knees and hips. Avalement was developed by French ski racers as a means of keeping their skis in constant contact with the snow on grooved and bumpy race courses.

As it helped the racers from being thrust airborne by the moguls, so avalement can help all skiers keep their skis on the surface on any uneven ski run and slope. In fact, basic avalement may be the most useful advanced skiing manoeuvre for all levels of skiers and should become second nature when passing over bumps at high or medium speeds.

1 Basic avalement

If you were driving in the car of your dreams on a bumpy road, you would probably be very upset if the entire chassis went up and down each time the car passed over a bump. Indeed, you would probably bring the car back to the dealer to have the suspension system overhauled. What you would expect, in fact, is that the suspension springs would compress and absorb the bump as the wheel passed over it and that the suspension springs would extend again having passed over the bump so that the chassis would remain quiet and still, regardless of the road condition.

To help understand avalement it is useful to look at a simplified car suspension system (fig 10) and understand what is happening. The chassis of a car constantly exerts a downward force causing the wheels to press against the road surface. As the wheel meets the bump, the bump pushes up against the wheel which starts to compress the suspension spring. The chassis attitude remains constant. As the wheel approaches the peak of the bump, the spring continues to compress and is most compressed at the summit of the bump. As the wheel starts to descend the bump, the spring begins to extend back to the neutral position and is completely neutral when the wheel fully descends the bump and is back on the flat surface.

Fig 11 shows how the body can be compared to a car for the purpose of analogy. If you think of your head and torso as the 'chassis', your hips, knees and legs as the 'suspension springs' and the skis as the 'wheels', then we can make a direct comparison with the previous example.

Your 'chassis' is heavy and is constantly exerting a downward force. As your skis reach a mogul, they should push up against your 'suspension system' and the 'suspension system' should compress. This means that your knees should push up towards your chest with your hip as the pivot point. Obviously this will not occur if your knees and hips are rigid. What will happen instead is that your entire body will ride up over the mogul and, if you are skiing fast, you will become airborne as you shoot off the top of the mogul. So keep your knees and hips relaxed to allow the moguls to compress the knees.

As you start to pass over the back of the

Fig 10. Suspension springs compressing and extending as car passes over a bump in the road.

mogul, push your feet downwards making sure you keep your skis in constant contact with the snow. When you have descended the mogul your legs and knees should be back in a relaxed position.

Special tips

● So that you are not thrown backwards when your knees are thrust upwards by the mogul, when skiing avalement on a packed-snow slope you should sit slightly lower and bend slightly forward from the waist so that your centre of gravity is always over the middle of the ski boots. (Picture 71a shows a normal piste traverse position and 71b shows the body modification required for avalement skiing.)

Basic traverse position.   71a

● Always keep your shins leaning against the fronts of the ski boots.

● Resist the temptation to lower your hips as you pass over the mogul. It is not the hips that go down, but the knees that are pushed up!

● Avalement turns can be performed either with your weight equally spread over both skis, or with the weight shifting from ski to ski.

● Some of my students have found it easier to visualize avalement if they think of it as a 'pumping' motion of the knees. The knees pump up as you ski up the mogul and pump down as you ski down the mogul.

Modified body position for skiing avalement over   71b
moguls.

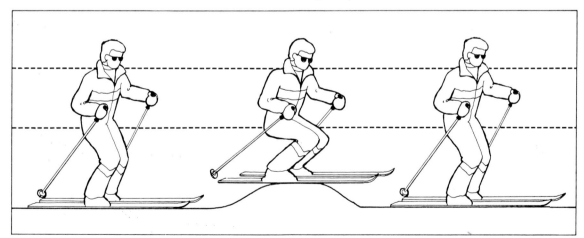

Fig 11. As the body passes over a mogul, during avalement the knees are 'pushed up' towards the chest, 'swallowing' the mogul.

2 Avalement while traversing

Prior to learning the avalement turn it is a good idea to practise traversing across a mogul field, passing over the tops of each mogul in your path and 'swallowing' each mogul as you ride up, over and down it, so as to keep your skis in total contact with the snow. Even if you decide not to learn avalement turns, knowing how to absorb moguls with your knees at high speeds (or out-of-control speeds) can be very useful and should be learnt by every skier.

The following exercises should be performed on an easy intermediate slope

---

A Shallow traverse over small moguls

The best learning sequence is to start with moguls that are not too large and then advance to large moguls. Choose a shallow traverse track that will take you over a series of small moguls. Keep your weight mostly over your downhill ski (picture 72a). At all times press down, but keep your knees and hips relaxed.

Start to traverse and, as you reach the first mogul, assume an avalement-modified position and allow the mogul to compress your knees so that they are fully compressed at the top of the mogul (picture 72b). As you start to descend the mogul press your feet downwards and extend your legs to keep your skis in contact with the snow (picture 72c). Throughout the manoeuvre, maintain a good traverse position with most of your weight on the instep of your downhill ski boot and with the skis well edged. Repeat on the opposite side.

72a

72c

72a–c: Avalement while traversing mogul field.

72b

B   Steeper traverse over small moguls

On the same slope, choose a steeper traverse track on a short mogul field that passes over a series of small moguls, and repeat the avalement movements. Repeat again on a very steep traverse, being certain that you have sufficient space after the short mogul field to regain control if necessary. Repeat on the opposite side.

C   Shallow traverse over large moguls

Repeat exercise 2A, choosing a shallow traverse track that passes over a series of large moguls. Repeat on the other side.

D   Steeper traverse over large moguls

Repeat exercise 2B, over large moguls.

The following exercises are to be performed on an advanced intermediate slope

---

When you feel confident skiing avalement traverses on the intermediate slopes, execute the same manoeuvres on a more difficult slope.

E   Shallow traverse over small moguls

Choose a shallow traverse that passes over a series of small moguls and repeat the avalement movements on both sides, as in exercise 2A.

F   Steeper traverse over large moguls

Repeat exercise 2B, passing over large moguls.

Note

□   When you attempt to ski avalement on a steep traverse track over large moguls (exercise 2F) on steep runs, you will probably be hitting each mogul very hard and your knees may be driven with considerable force into your chest. I therefore recommend this exercise only for those of you who are very fit, very daring, and who are feeling very confident using avalement. I also recommend that you choose a very short mogul field with a large smooth runout beyond the moguls.

3   Avalement turns

When you have mastered swallowing up the moguls with your legs, you will be ready to turn your skis using avalement. When making an avalement turn you ski across, and start your turn on, the summit of the mogul, and steer your skis through the turn as you descend on the back of the mogul. It is best to make uphill turns before learning to turn the skis downhill across the fall-line. It is also advisable to practise first on an easy intermediate slope and then, once the manoeuvre is mastered, to move on to an advanced intermediate slope.

A   Avalement turn uphill–starting on a steep traverse

Start on a steep traverse on an easy intermediate slope holding your uphill ski pole vertical and aim for a medium-sized mogul (picture 73a). As you ride up the mogul, plant your ski pole on the summit of the mogul and swallow the mogul as you did in the previous exercises. When you reach the summit of the mogul and your knees are most compressed (picture 73b), turn your knees and feet uphill. As you ride over the crest of the mogul start extending your legs while you descend the back of the mogul (picture 73c), push your uphill hand forward to recover your ski pole and continue steering your skis up the hill (as shown in picture 73d), finishing in a good traverse position. Repeat this on the opposite side.

Special tips

● Keep your upper body facing down the hill throughout the turn.

● Initiating the turning of the skis at the summit of the mogul is very easy and is similar to the foot swivel manoeuvre (exercise 5E, page 81), since only the part of the ski beneath your feet is making contact with the snow.

● When making turns to the hill, keep most of your weight on the instep of your downhill ski boot.

73a

73b

B Avalement turn uphill—turning from the fall-line

This time, start by pointing your skis straight down the fall-line and repeat the same manoeuvre as above. As you start to ride up the mogul, bring one ski pole forward and prepare to plant it at the summit of the mogul (picture 74a). Arriving at the summit of the mogul, plant your ski pole and turn your skis uphill (picture 74b) as you did in the previous exercise, turning around the ski pole. Complete the turn by extending your legs as you descend the back of the mogul (picture 74c), push your hand forward to recover your ski pole and continue steering your skis up the hill to a smooth stop (picture 74d).

Special tips

- Since this is a very dynamic manoeuvre, you must be sure to be in the modified traverse position (picture 74b) with your upper body bent slightly forward at the waist, so that you are not thrown backwards when the mogul compresses your knees.

- Be sure to push your wrist forward as you pass your ski pole, in order that the ski pole does not pull your arm back resulting in an improper traverse position at the end of the turn.

- Practise this with your weight on the outside ski, and then with your weight over both skis.

73a–d: Avalement turn uphill.   73c

73d

74a

74b

74a–d: Avalement turn from fall-line with pole plant. 74c

74d

C Avalement turn downhill

On the same slope that you have used for the previous exercises, ski towards a large mogul in a steep traverse. As you start to ride up the mogul bring your downhill ski pole forward, ready to plant on the side of the mogul (picture 75a). As you arrive at the summit of the mogul, plant your ski pole at the summit and transfer your weight to the outside ski (picture 75b). Turn your skis downhill across the fall-line, steering with your knees and feet in the same way that you did for the uphill turn and push your wrist forward (picture 75c). Continue steering your skis across the fall-

line, turning them up the hill (picture 75d). End in a good traverse position ready for the next turn (picture 75e). Repeat, making a turn downhill in the opposite direction.

Special tip

● Be sure to keep your upper body bent slightly forward at the waist and constantly facing down the fall-line during the turn over the mogul.

75a

75b

75c

75d

75a–e: Avalement turn downhill (see previous page). 75e

4 Linked avalement turns

Once you can make avalement turns to both sides, it is very easy to link the turns. The key to linking turns is to ensure that you are in a good traverse position at the end of the turn so that you are in control to start the next turn.

Choose a field of small moguls on an easy intermediate slope to practise on, and link a series of avalement turns over the moguls. When you can ski these moguls with good control choose a mogul field with larger moguls and link some series of avalement turns. The next step is to practise on an advanced intermediate slope with small moguls and then finally ski through a field of large moguls on this slope making controlled avalement turns.

Wedeln turns

The wedeln turn, which the French and Swiss call the *Godille*, is essentially a shortswing turn executed quickly with the skis held close together, the weight on both feet at all times, very little down-up-down movement and with very little edging. The wedeln turn is mainly performed on gentle, smooth slopes or during acrobatic descents of mogul fields ('hot-dogging') when one tries to make as many turns as possible. Usually, advanced skiers build their egos by wedelning on the beginners' slopes.

Learning to wedeln can be done via a number of different approaches. I learnt to wedeln by rapidly 'hopping' my ski tails from side to side across the fall-line. Another approach is to ski with almost flat skis and accelerate the shortswing turn. I prefer to teach the wedeln turn by having the student develop a feeling for 'foot power', which is extremely useful when performing all skiing manoeuvres. I like to think of this as similar to driving a car with front-wheel drive (initiating the turn with the feet) rather than rear-wheel drive (initiating the turn with the knees, hips or upper body), which naturally, since there are fewer linkages to pass through, is quicker and more responsive. When you put the power in the feet, you have instant control of your skis.

Learning foot power

To master the foot power required for wedelning, start on an uncrowded, gentle slope and face your upper body down the fall-line. Spread your skis 10–20 cm (4–8 in) apart and point them just off the fall-line on a steep traverse. Hold your arms in the 'tray holding' position and lower your hips a little more than usual, so that you are sitting slightly with your knees relaxed and with your weight *evenly spread* over the middle of both feet, as shown in picture 76a.

Start to glide and, using only your feet, turn your skis *rapidly* from side to side as you descend the fall-line (pictures 76b, 76c and 76d). It's fun to count your turns and try to make as many as possible. If you are on a short slope, ride back up

the lift and repeat this manoeuvre until you feel that you are turning and controlling your skis using only your feet. Now begin to smooth out the turns by slowing down the tempo of the turning movements and with each descent start to bring your skis closer together. Eventually you should be able to place your skis together and, using only as much foot power as is necessary, smoothly, elegantly and unhurriedly wedeln down the fall-line.

Special tips

- Though the skis must roll slightly from edge to edge, try to keep them quite flat on the snow.

- Face your upper body down the fall-line the entire time.

- Keep your body relaxed and do not think about doing down-up-down movements.

76a

When you feel confident wedelning on the gentle slopes, you can try it on intermediate slopes, skiing a very narrow path down the run. When you feel very confident on the smooth intermediate slopes and you want to 'hot-dog', you can wedeln while descending mogul fields.

Note

□ The word *wedeln* comes from Austria and means the 'wagging' of a dog's tail. So, be true to the name and try to wedeln with quick, fluid motions.

76b

76c

76a–d (inc. overleaf): Learning 'foot power' for making wedeln turns.

76d

The stem turn for intermediate and advanced skiers

(skiing crusty snow conditions)

This is a manoeuvre which I find especially valuable when skiing off the packed slopes on crusty snow that has a tendency to break beneath the skis. It enables you to turn your skis with a minimum of down-up-down movements, and uses instead gentle weight transfer movements which help prevent the skis from breaking through the crusty snow surface. I also like this manoeuvre when skiing 'off-piste' when there are windblown ridges. (A very different way of skiing these crusty conditions is the jump turn, which is explained in Section Three.)

The stem turn for crusty snow conditions

This exercise should be practised on packed snow and then applied to crusty snow.

Choose an easy intermediate packed slope and start in a shallow traverse with your weight evenly distributed on both skis (picture 77a). When you are ready to make a downhill turn, place more weight on your downhill ski and gently slide (or step) the back of your uphill ski out to the side, changing the ski edge by rolling your knee inwards (picture 77b). Keep the front of the skis fairly close together and lean against the fronts of both ski boots. When you push (or lift) this ski to the side you should have little weight on the ski. As the stepped (outside) ski crosses the fall-line begin to shift your weight gently on to this ski (pictures 77c and 77d), testing, as you do so, the firmness of the snow beneath the skis.

If the snow seems capable of supporting you, continue to gently transfer your weight on to this ski (picture 77e) and continue steering the ski across the fall-line until it starts to point uphill.

Special tips

● When skiing on the crust, if the snow does not feel firm and starts to break when you begin to shift your weight on to the outside ski, remove the weight from the stepping ski by placing your weight again over your downhill (inside) ski, bring the stepping ski back alongside the downhill ski and continue to traverse, looking for another place to initiate the turn.

● Do not be anxious to bring your inside ski parallel to the outside ski, but rather allow it to trail behind as your skis cross the fall-line.

When you feel in control, with your weight mostly on the instep of your new downhill ski and your ski turning up the hill, start to slide the uphill ski parallel to the downhill ski and roll your uphill knee outwards. Now distribute your weight again evenly over both skis and finish in a good traverse position (picture 77f).

Notes

□ The stem turn should be performed only at slow or moderate speeds.

□ There is very little flexion-extension-flexion unweighting in this manoeuvre when performed in 'off-piste' snow conditions. (There naturally is a nuance of such movement as you transfer your weight from ski to ski.) Picture sequence 78 demonstrates how the stem turn can be employed to ski a windblown, crusty slope. Notice how the weight shifts gradually to the outside ski and how the inside ski is brought parallel well *after* the skis have crossed the fall-line.

□ The standard stem turn, as taught by many ski schools to beginners, generally emphasizes the unweighting movement. These ski schools teach the standard stem turn as a step in the progression to learning to ski parallel. My observations through the years are that beginners who have been taught the standard stem turn tend to remain stem skiers and find it difficult to move on to parallel skiing. While I believe that there is nothing potentially dangerous or wrong about skiers using the stem turn as their standard turn, I feel that it is not graceful, unlike the parallel turn, it cannot safely be performed at high speed, and the body movements required to make the stem turn do not integrate naturally with the movements required to perform many of the advanced skiing manoeuvres. In my opinion one should already be a reasonably good parallel skier before learning the stem turn, and then should only use the stem turn in particular situations.

77b

77a

77c

77d

77e

77f

77a–f: Stem turn on packed slope.

78b

78a

78c

78d

78a–f: Stem turn on windblown crust.

78e

78f

The jet turn

The jet turn is another skiing manoeuvre developed by ski racers to help them get their skis through the turns faster, and was very popular during the early 1970s as recreational skiers tried to emulate the 'sitting back' styles of the top racers. While the jet turn has lost a lot of its popularity as a racing manoeuvre, it is extremely useful to advanced and intermediate skiers who, for all sorts of reasons, occasionally find themselves thrown backwards against the backs of their boots with a consequent loss of control of their skis. The jet turn manoeuvre teaches you how to bring your weight forward again and regain control so that you can end the turn in a correct position, leaning against the fronts of the ski boots. The jet turn is also an enjoyable ski manoeuvre when you're playing around on the moguls.

The major difference between the jet turn and the basic flexion-extension-flexion turn is that instead of extending your upper body (as you do for the basic turn), for the jet turn you extend your lower body. You do this by shooting (or accelerating) your skis forward and towards the direction of the turn (as can be seen in pictures 81c, 81d and 81e).

When you shoot your skis forward, you end up leaning against the backs of the ski boots (picture 81d). Therefore in order to maintain control as you come out of the turn it is essential that you recover your correct position by pulling with your stomach muscles and pushing hard off your ski pole so that your body recovers to a position with your weight over the middle of your ski boots and with your shins leaning against the fronts of the boots (picture 81f).

Special tip

● When skiing on packed slopes, the jet turn is used exclusively for skiing moguls and is not normally employed on the smooth parts of the slope except as a recovery tactic. It is therefore advisable to learn the jet turn on moguls.

Prior to learning the jet turn across the fall-line it is best to learn how to accelerate the skis forward. This you can do by traversing across a series of moguls and accelerating your skis off the summit of each mogul in the direction of the traverse.

1 Accelerating skis forward while traversing

Choose a traverse track that will bring you over a series of small moguls on an easy intermediate

79a

79b

79c

slope, as shown in picture 79a. Start traversing, and, as you approach the first mogul, start flexing (lowering) your hips as you do for the basic down-up-down turn and prepare to plant your ski pole at the summit of the mogul (picture 79b). From your lowest flexed position at the top of the mogul, shoot your skis forward in the same traverse direction.

This will result in your legs extending and being thrust against the backs of your ski boots and you will be supporting yourself momentarily with your ski pole (picture 79c). As soon as you have shot your skis forward, push off your ski pole and bring your body forward again so that you end up in the correct traverse position over the middle of your ski boots and leaning against the fronts of the ski boots (picture 79d). Repeat this manoeuvre as you ski over each mogul. Repeat in the opposite direction.

When you have mastered shooting your skis forward and recovering your position by pushing off your ski pole, you are ready to make jet turns.

2 Jet turn uphill

It is usually a good idea to learn to perform new manoeuvres by turning uphill before making turns across the fall-line (downhill).

On an easy intermediate slope, start off on a steep traverse towards a small mogul, as shown in picture 80a. Bring your *uphill* ski pole vertical and, as you did in the previous exercise, plant it on the summit of the mogul as you flex (lower) your hips (picture 80b). Since you want to turn your skis uphill, as you shoot your skis forward steer your skis uphill by turning your feet and knees uphill (picture 80c). Now push off your ski pole to bring your body forward and continue to keep the skis turning uphill (picture 80d). Finish the uphill turn in a good traverse position with your weight balanced over the centre of your ski boots (picture 80e).

79a–d: Jetting skis forward during traverse across mogul.   79d

Special tip

● It is easiest to ski jet turns with your weight evenly distributed over both skis at all times.

80a   80b

80c

80a–e: Jet turn uphill.   80d

3   Jet turn across the fall-line

In picture sequence 81 I am performing an *exaggerated* jet turn across the fall-line in order to emphasize visually the extension of the lower body. (When performing the jet turn it is not necessary to exaggerate as much as this.) As recommended for all of the learning sequences, start with small moguls on easy intermediate slopes and gradually progress on to large moguls on advanced intermediate slopes.

Choose an easy intermediate slope and, starting in a good traverse position on a shallow traverse, ski towards a small mogul, as in picture 81a. As you approach the mogul bring your *downhill* ski pole forward so that it is ready to be planted, and start lowering your hips (picture 81b). As you arrive at the summit of the mogul, plant your ski pole and begin to shoot your skis forward (picture 81c). Since you want to turn your skis down the hill, as you shoot your skis forward (picture 81d), steer them in the direction of the turn with your knees and feet so that the skis cross over the fall-line (picture 81e). Now push off your ski pole and bring your body forward over your skis so that you are in a good traverse position with your shins against the fronts of your ski boots as you complete the turn (picture 81f).

Repeat this manoeuvre on the opposite side, and then progress to bigger moguls and steeper slopes.

When you can perform jet turns confidently on both sides and can link the turns together, enjoy yourself by skiing down some mogul fields, jet turning off the moguls.

80e

81c

81b

81a

81d

Notes

☐ If you plan on being a powder snow skier, it is a good idea to perfect your jet turn because it is an excellent way of turning your skis in deep powder snow. In fact, I almost always employ jet turns when I'm powder skiing in evergreen glades to turn my skis around the trees. Naturally in deep powder you cannot lean on your ski pole as you can on a packed slope, so you must modify the extension of the lower body as you accelerate the skis into the turn and use more stomach muscle power to help bring your body forward at the end of the turn. Skiing powder snow with the jet turn is covered in Section Three.

☐ The jet turn is also a very good way to initiate turns in heavy, wet and crusty snow.

81a–f: Exaggerated jet turn over mogul.

81e

81f

The racing step
(lateral step)

The French call this the *Godille Performant*, but I refer to it as the racing step, as this gives a clearer visual image of the manoeuvre to most people, including those who understand French. As the name suggests, this is a high-speed manoeuvre used at times by racers to change ski edges as they turn through the gates on a racecourse.

The major difference between this and a shortswing turn is that during the racing step, the skis are not permitted to make a large, sweeping turn. The idea is to keep the skis pointed down the fall-line as much as possible in order not to lose speed when going from one turn to the next. The way this is accomplished is by putting all your weight over the edge of the downhill ski so that you have complete control of this ski, and pumping and thrusting your legs as you push off

this edge in order to step laterally on to the edge of the outside ski, ensuring maximum control as you steer through the turn. During the racing step, the actions of shifting from ski edge to ski edge are rapid and explosive, and consequently are physically as well as technically demanding.

Although you may have no intention of ski racing, you should learn this manoeuvre because it provides excellent, precise control at the high speeds that advanced skiers often like to ski. It is also a useful way to ski under control through a mogul field at high speeds.

1 The racing step on a smooth slope

Prior to practising the racing step, review the skating exercises starting on page 49 of Section One. Practise skating straight down the fall-line using exaggerated down-up-down movements. The body movements required for the racing

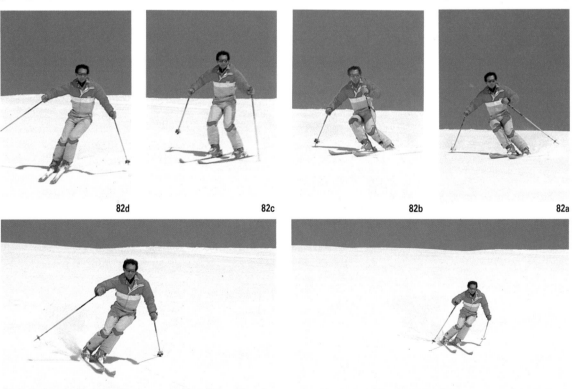

82d   82c   82b   82a

82a–f: Racing step on smooth slope.   82e   82f

step are essentially the same as for skating. The main difference is that instead of pointing the tip of the ski *up* the hill as you thrust laterally on to the outside edge (as you do when skating), during the racing step you point the ski tip *towards* the fall-line and thrust and shift your body laterally on to the inside edge.

Choose a smooth stretch on a gentle slope. Start skiing on a steep traverse with your weight completely on your downhill ski (picture 82a). When you are ready to turn, lower your hips and start to plant your downhill ski pole (picture 82b). As you push off the ski edge, pump your leg in order to thrust your body laterally across the fall-line (picture 82c), roll your outside knee in the direction of the turn, and rapidly transfer your weight on to the inside edge of your outside ski (picture 82d).

As your weight transfers on to the new ski, lean your upper body so as to put all the body weight on the outside (control) ski (picture 82e). To help put your weight over the outside ski, you can lift the tail of the inside ski slightly. Keep the skis well edged, press your shins firmly against the fronts of the ski boots and steer the ski through the turn with your knee and foot. When you are ready for the next turn, start to lower your hips, plant your downhill ski pole and prepare to push off again to execute the turn across the fall-line (picture 82f).

Special tips

- Try to maintain a smooth rhythm as you link racing steps down the slope.

- As you push off the edge of your ski and rapidly transfer your weight to your outside ski, the tail of your pushing ski may momentarily trail behind as your outside ski starts to turn across the fall-line. By keeping your shins pressed against the fronts of your ski boots you will easily be able to bring this ski parallel to the outside ski as you complete the turn.

- Notice in picture sequence 82 how the upper body faces down the fall-line throughout the turn, and is used to keep the weight balanced over the inside edge of the control ski.

2 The racing step on moguls

If you are doing the racing step correctly you should have excellent control of your skis at high speeds. You are therefore ready to apply the racing step to skiing moguls.

Special tip

- This manoeuvre is quite the opposite approach to skiing a mogul field using the counter-turn (Section Two, page 104), and requires you to ski aggressively and dynamically while constantly applying pressure to the fronts of your ski boots.

On an easy intermediate slope, ski on a steep traverse track towards a mogul with all your weight on your downhill ski (picture 83a). As you approach the mogul lower your hip, plant your downhill ski pole and push hard off the side of the mogul (picture 83b), pumping your legs so that your weight shifts laterally across the fall-line on to the inside edge of your outside ski (picture 83c) as you turn your skis around the mogul. With all your weight on the inside edge of this new downhill ski aim for the side of the next mogul and immediately begin flexing and preparing for the next turn (picture 83d).

Continue down the slope, keeping close to the fall-line and making racing turns around the moguls.

83a

83b

83c

83a–d (inc. prev. page): Using the racing step to turn around moguls.

83d

3　The racing step on steeper slopes

A　Smooth slope

When you feel confident at the speeds attained skiing the racing step on gentle slopes, practise skiing the racing step on steeper slopes, concentrating on maintaining complete control of the skis at all times.

B　Moguls

When you feel confident and in control on the steeper, smooth slopes choose a steep slope with moguls and practise skiing the racing step through these larger moguls at higher speeds.

Note

☐ If you wish to ski slower when using the racing step to turn around moguls all you need do is ride the edge of your outside ski longer, steering your skis so that they turn further from the fall-line (up the hill) as you pass around the mogul. This is also known as a lateral projection turn. The maxim to remember is: the faster you want to ski, the closer you should keep your skis to the fall-line; the slower you want to ski, the more your skis should turn from the fall-line.

Simple acrobatics

Ballet and acrobatic skiing have now become disciplines with quite a number of devotees. They are very beautiful to watch and fun to do once you have learnt the movements. Many of the ballet and acrobatic manoeuvres require lots of practice in order to perform them gracefully and safely. However, there are a number of simple manoeuvres that are easy to perform and that I recommend for advanced skiers as, apart from being enjoyable, they help to achieve better balance and perfect edge control. In addition, a number of the manoeuvres require skiing on the uphill edge of the uphill ski, which is extremely useful to help advanced skiers learn independent leg action.

Because a top skier should be equally able to ski on the downhill ski, uphill ski or on both skis, I recommend that you practise some of these acrobatics to enhance your balance and control.

By practising some of the simple jumping manoeuvres you will learn to control your skis in the air and help improve the feeling between your body and your skis. Furthermore, you will learn how to land correctly so that should you accidentally be tossed airborne by a mogul or unexpected drop off, the consequences need not be disastrous.

84a

84b

1 Skiing on the uphill edge of the uphill ski

Since a number of the acrobatics require skiing on the uphill edge of the uphill ski it is best to start by learning how to do this simple manoeuvre.

A Traversing on the uphill edge

Choose a gentle slope that is not crowded. Assume a proper traverse position and begin skiing on a very shallow traverse. As you pick up speed, lean your body up the hill, keep your knees bent and lift your downhill ski out to the side (holding the ski parallel to the ground) until you have your weight balanced over the uphill edge of the uphill ski (pictures 84a, 84b and 84c).

Continue traversing in this manner and stop. Repeat on the opposite side.

84a–c: Traversing on uphill edge of uphill ski. 84c

B Sidesliding to a stop on uphill edge

When you can perform exercise A comfortably on both sides, choose a slightly steeper traverse track on the same slope and repeat the procedure. When you are ready to stop, flatten the uphill ski slightly, turn the ski uphill (steer with your knee and foot) and sideslide to a stop (picture sequence 85). Repeat on the opposite side.

C Turning uphill on the uphill edge (with no sideslide)

On a similar traverse track to exercise B, repeat the same procedure. Instead of sidesliding to a stop, keep your ski on its edge and steer it with your knee and foot up the hill to a stop (picture sequence 86). Repeat this traverse and uphill turn on both sides until you have mastered the technique.

85a

86a

85b

86b

85c

86c

85a–c: Sidesliding to a stop on uphill edge of uphill ski.   86a–c: Turning uphill on uphill edge of uphill ski.

2   The Charleston Ski Dance

This is a manoeuvre which Art Furrer, a Swiss ski acrobat, developed in the early 1960s and I've had lots of fun with it ever since. Apart from using it to show off on easy slopes, it is a delightful way to 'dance' down a field of small moguls. Once you can ski on the uphill edge of your uphill ski this manoeuvre is easy; it is only a matter of learning the timing and rhythm.

A   Charleston on a smooth slope

Start as I do in picture 87a, in other words, in a steep traverse track on a gentle slope with your weight on your uphill ski and with the tail of your downhill ski lifted in the air to the side. Begin to slide, and almost immediately swing the ski that is in the air beneath you (picture 87b), and transfer your weight on to the inside edge of this ski as it makes contact with the snow (picture 87c), simultaneously swinging the tail of the other ski off the snow and to the side. As you glide on this edge, continue to turn uphill, start swinging your other ski beneath you and again transfer your weight on to this ski edge as it makes contact with the snow.

Special tips

● This is a ski dance and can only be done with a constant steady rhythm; as one ski tail swings down the other ski tail swings up.

● Until you master this movement, keep the fronts of both skis in the snow at all times. (When you become very good ski dancing the Charleston, you can swing the entire ski in the air.)

● The Charleston can be performed with or without ski poles. When using your ski poles, plant your ski pole simultaneously with your ski swing. As the swinging ski makes contact with the snow, plant the ski pole, as shown in picture 87c.

● Try to keep your upper body fairly still and facing down the fall-line the entire time. Note in picture sequence 87 that the upper body remains fixed as the skis swing beneath it.

87a

87b

87a–c: Charleston Ski Dance on smooth slope.   87c

88a

88b

88a–c: Charleston Ski Dance through mogul field.

88c

B Charleston around moguls

Once you feel relaxed skiing the Charleston on a smooth slope, it is good fun to Charleston around the moguls.

Choose a short series of moguls on a gentle or intermediate slope and practise the same Charleston movements that you did on the smooth slope, making each turn on the uphill edge of your uphill ski and turning around the moguls. Picture sequence 88 shows the Charleston Ski Dance through a mogul field.

3 The Butterfly (or royal christie)

I've heard this manoeuvre referred to as both the butterfly and the royal christie. Since I learnt it as the butterfly, and also because this is a more vivid name, I'll refer to it as this. The butterfly is a very impressive manoeuvre for spectators and yet is very easy to perform since it is nothing more than a combination of skiing on the uphill edge of the uphill ski and skating.

Notes

☐ As in many of the simple acrobatics, the difficulty is in getting the rhythm started. However, once you get reasonably good at the manoeuvre it will become easier to get quickly into the rhythm.

☐ Prior to learning to place one ski behind your head (picture sequence 90), it is best to first practise combining skating across the fall-line while skiing on the uphill edge of the uphill ski.

A Practice with ski lifted to the side

Start on a medium traverse track on a gentle slope and traverse with your weight on the uphill edge of your uphill ski (picture 89a). As you gain momentum, roll on to the downhill edge of the uphill ski (picture 89b), and step across the fall-line on to the uphill edge of the opposite ski (picture 89c), leaning your body uphill and holding the downhill ski horizontally out to the side parallel with the ground. Glide on this ski as you cross the slope (picture 89d) and come to a stop. Repeat in the opposite direction and then practise linking the turns without stopping.

89a

89b

89c

89d

89a–d: Skating across fall-line on to inside ski, holding outside ski in the air.

90a   90b

90c

B   Butterfly position

Once you have mastered skating across the fall-line holding the outside ski horizontally in the air, it is only a matter of courage to place the ski behind your back.

Start performing the manoeuvre exactly as for exercise 3A (as shown in pictures 90a and 90b). As you step across the fall-line on to the uphill edge of the uphill ski, rather than holding your downhill leg to the side, bend your downhill knee and place this ski behind your back (picture 90c).

90a–d: Butterfly turns to right.   90d

Special tip

● It helps to bend from the waist so that your back is horizontal and parallel to the ground (picture 90d).

Glide across the slope in this butterfly position and steer to a stop.

Repeat on the opposite side and then practise linking the turns without stopping between turns.

Notes

☐ Butterfly turns should be skied without planting your ski poles.

☐ When you feel comfortable skiing butterfly turns on both sides you can impress your friends by skiing down a gentle slope linking a series of butterfly turns.

☐ If you become proficient and are daring, it is easy to ski a mogul field making butterfly turns around the moguls.

4   A simple jump turn over a mogul

A jump turn off a mogul is fun and very easy to perform. All you have to do is make the basic intermediate turn over a mogul with increased speed, extending with a strong leg thrust.

Approach a mogul on an easy intermediate slope with more speed than you would normally ski if you didn't wish to be thrown airborne. Flex (lower) your hips as you would for the normal down-up-down turn and plant your downhill ski pole on the up-slope of the mogul (picture 91a). As you start to ride up the mogul forcefully thrust your legs upwards and start your turn around your downhill ski pole.

As you crest the mogul you will find that your violent upthrust motion and your increased speed have caused your skis to 'fly' off the mogul so that they are no longer in contact with the snow (picture 91b). Continue turning your skis in the air across the fall-line (picture 91c) and land in the new direction in a correct traverse position with your weight over the instep of your downhill ski boot (picture 91d). When you are in the air your legs should be extended and as you land you should absorb the landing shock by flexing (lowering) your hips and knees. Now traverse to a stop. Practise jumping off moguls in both directions.

When you feel comfortable jump turning to both sides, link the jump turns, concentrating on landing softly and in control. When this becomes easy, increase your speed and try to jump over two moguls (picture sequence 92) as you turn your skis in the air. If the moguls are sufficiently close together and you have enough speed you may even be able to jump over several.

Special tip

● Survey the jump and time it carefully so that you always land in the trough behind a mogul or on the back slope of a mogul, as it can be quite painful landing on the up-slope or the top of a mogul.

91b

91a

91a–d: Jump turn over mogul.

91c

91d

92a

92b

92c

92a–d: Jump turn over two moguls.   92d

5 Two-pole tuck jump over a mogul

This is a simple manoeuvre to execute and is impressive when performed over large moguls. During this manoeuvre the legs are tucked up towards the chest while the skis are in the air, as shown in picture 93b. The tuck jump can be executed with or without turns. I enjoy making tuck jump turns on advanced slopes over large moguls at slow speeds. I usually employ the tuck jump without a turn for jumping off corniches or drop-offs into deep powder snow.

A Straight tuck jump

Practise on an intermediate slope. Ski towards a medium-sized mogul on a shallow traverse. As you approach the mogul place your hands on the tops of your ski poles and, as you flex (lower) your hips, plant *both* ski poles near the top of the mogul, as shown in picture 93a. Now spring up with a strong leg extension, pushing off both feet, and simultaneously push down on your ski poles so that your arms are lifted straight over the poles. As you become airborne, lift your knees towards your chest (picture 93b). Start to straighten your legs prior to landing and land in control in a traverse position (picture 93c), and then flex your knees and hips to absorb the landing impact. Practise this manoeuvre in both directions and jump over progressively larger moguls.

B Tuck jump with turns

On an intermediate slope, ski a shallow traverse track towards a medium-sized mogul. As you approach the mogul lower your hips, plant both ski poles near the summit (picture 94a) and spring up (in the same way as for the straight tuck jump) and initiate a turn around your downhill ski pole (picture 94b). As you become airborne tuck your knees up towards your chest and continue turning your skis in the air across the fall-line (picture 94c). Straighten your legs prior to landing and land in control in the new direction in a correct traverse position with your weight on the instep of the downhill ski boot (picture 94d). Absorb the landing impact with flexed knees and hips, and ski to a stop. Practise this on both sides.

93a–c: Straight tuck jump over mogul.

94a

When you feel confident making the two-pole tuck jump turn over the medium-sized moguls, gradually choose larger moguls to jump turn over and then perform the manoeuvre on steeper slopes.

Special tips

- The trick is to be certain to land in good control and to absorb the landing with flexible knees and hips.

- Keep your back straight and relaxed.

- Always try to land on the back of a mogul, or on a steep pitch on a slope, or in the trough between moguls. Never intentionally land on the up-slope nor on the top of a mogul.

- For all jumps it is very important that you land with your skis parallel to the landing pitch.

94b

94c

94a–d: Two-pole tuck jump turn over mogul.   94d

95a–e: Split jump off mogul.   95a 95b

6 The split jump (spread eagle)

Jumping off big moguls, corniches and specially prepared jumps has become very popular among young skiers, but there are many acrobatic jumps and flips that are potentially very dangerous if not performed correctly. I prefer to leave all flips to those ski acrobats who are performing in ski jumping competitions. (The only flips I have ever done have always been unintentional and I've always managed to land upended!) However, jumping off moguls keeping your skis beneath you is easy, fun and safe.

My favourite jump, and also that of many of my students over the years, has been the split jump, which looks as if it is painful on landing, but is actually very easy to perform correctly. Once you can jump and land correctly doing the split jump, you will have the basic skill to perform any number of other jumps where you keep your head more or less above your skis. These include the 'Daffy', 'Mulekick', 'Crossed Backscratcher', 'Side Twist', and 'Tip-drop', to name but a few of the more common ones shown in pictures 96a–96e. How big a mogul you choose to jump over depends on your youth, courage and ability.

To perform the split jump, choose a mogul that has a smooth, moderately steep pitch behind it or jump off a specially prepared small jump with a moderately steep landing pitch.

Ski towards the mogul and plant your ski pole as you lower your hips (picture 95a). As you

95d

95e

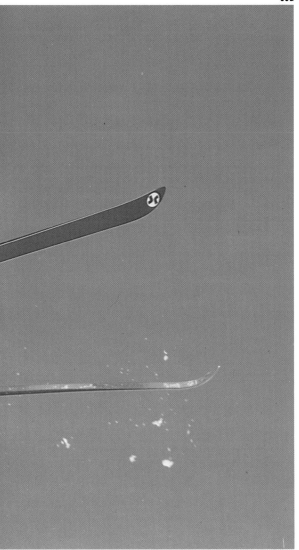

95c

approach the top of the mogul spring off the mogul with a strong leg extension (picture 95b) pushing off with both feet and, as you are going up in the air, spread your skis wide apart (picture 95c) and at the same time spread your arms apart for balance. As you pass the apex of the jump bring your legs together and lower your arms to maintain good balance (picture 95d). Keep your legs extended prior to landing and then absorb the landing impact by flexing your knees and lowering your hips (picture 95e).

Special tips

● The key to this manoeuvre is to be sure to bring your legs together as you start your descent towards the snow.

● Keep your back vertical and relaxed.

● Land with your skis parallel to the landing pitch.

Mulekick.

Daffy Jump.

Side Twist.

Tip-drop.

Crossed Backscratcher.

96a – e

Skiing the steep gullies and mountain faces

Skiing gullies and mountain faces is exciting, dangerous, stimulating, challenging, adventurous and superb fun! Each year more and more people are venturing off the packed slopes and on to these steep pitches. Two days after a light snowstorm in Val d'Isère, France—the reputed world capital for out-of-bounds ('off-piste') skiing—one can see tracks coming down every possible and seemingly impossible mountain face and gully. The challenge among these skiers is not speed of descent, but rather to get to their favourite gullies before too many others do. Skiing the mountain faces and gullies is one of my favourite skiing pleasures and can be yours, too, if skied with care and safety.

Although one often skis these steep pitches in powder snow over a firm base, it is also common to ski these same pitches on spring (transformed) snow. The technique for skiing 'the steep' in deep powder snow is covered in Section Three.

Skiing on the transformed snow, which can vary from frozen granular (hard and icy), to granular (just soft enough for the edges to grip), to sugar (light snow granules on a firm base), to corn (large, slightly wet snow granules on a firm base—also called 'ball bearings'), to mashed potatoes (wet snow on a soggy base), to concrete (very heavy, wet snow on very soft base), requires nothing more than a refinement of the techniques you have already learnt, and a daring nature.

Special tip

● I strongly recommend that you do not ski the steep slopes on frozen granular, mashed potatoes, or concrete snow, as these conditions are all very dangerous.

Because a fall on many of the steep gullies or mountain faces can be very painful or worse, it is best to practise your technique and control on short, steep pitches on the advanced intermediate or difficult slopes.

Obviously when skiing steep pitches, control is more important than style and therefore you should ski with your skis kept at whatever distance apart you feel most comfortable. Some skiers prefer to ski with their feet very close together, but I find that if you ski with independent leg action, with a space between your skis, you can often use the uphill ski to prevent you from falling should you lose control of your downhill ski.

To learn to ski the very steep slopes, choose a short steep pitch on a difficult run and pick a path down the centre so that if you lose control you will have enough runout to the sides to allow you to regain control. The object of this manoeuvre is to turn your skis 180° from one traverse to the next without picking up much momentum. There are various ways to accomplish this.

Sylvain Saudan, the master of 'Extreme Skiing', relies on very powerful thighs to thrust his skis across the fall-line. I was taught to jump my skis out of the snow, pivot them in the air and land on the edge of the downhill ski, facing in the new direction. (This movement causes the skier to break contact with the snow and then reestablish contact after the turn and also has the skier working against the pull of gravity.) Although there are certain times that I will use this manoeuvre, such as in extremely narrow gullies, I find an easy and sure way to turn one's skis in most circumstances is to combine extreme anticipation (page 99), banking and knee steering.

To perform this turn, choose a short steep pitch on an advanced intermediate slope. Start in a traverse position with your weight on the instep of your downhill ski, your skis sufficiently edged to prevent sideslipping and your upper body facing down the fall-line. Begin traversing (picture 97a) then immediately lower your hips and, using anticipation, plant your ski pole down the hill (picture 97b).

Now, rather than extending with a strong upthrust, make use of the strong pull of gravity

97a

97b

that is evident on these steep slopes by banking your turn (offsetting your weight by leaning in the direction of the pole plant) and then, using a slight hip extension, roll your knees downhill (picture 97c). As your ski tips begin to swing around, push your inside arm (pole-planting arm) forwards down the hill, transfer your weight to your new downhill ski (picture 97d), and continue to swing your knees across the fall-line (picture 97e), ready for the next turn. Be sure to press on the instep of the downhill foot to maintain good ski control and keep your upper body facing down the fall-line. Repeat the turn in the opposite direction.

When you feel comfortable making turns to both sides, choose a narrow path down the centre of the slope and imagine that you are in a very narrow gully with walls on each side, and limit yourself to skiing down this narrow width, turning your skis from side to side gaining as little speed as possible. Perform the same turns on a very steep advanced run, using extreme anticipation.

Notes

☐ When you feel confident skiing in total control on a very steep slope, you are probably ready to ski the 'off-piste' gullies and mountain faces. How well you progress from here depends very much on your nature, and even for those of you who are very daring, it is preferable for students of 'the steep' to progress gradually to the more dangerous slopes.

☐ Begin skiing 'off-piste' mountain faces that are wide and free of rocks and lead into snowbowls, so that should you fall you will stop gradually with little risk of serious injury.

☐ Gradually choose increasingly steeper slopes to descend.

☐ Start skiing short gullies that open on to wide slopes or snowbowls and then gradually progress to longer gullies.

☐ Only after you have put in many hours of skiing on the types of gullies and mountain faces recommended above should you attempt to ski gullies or mountain faces that cut above cliffs or large drop-offs.

☐ It is advisable to ski off-piste mountain faces and gullies in the company of ski instructors who specialize in off-piste skiing in that particular area, or with certified mountain guides.

97c

97d

97a–e: Turn on steep slope (skiing 'imaginary gully').

97e

Walking up slopes using skins

Skins attached to the bottoms of skis enable a skier to climb up a hill without slipping backwards–which is extremely useful for exploring the mountains beyond the limits of the lift-serviced ski areas.

Skins were originally made from seal pelts that have hairs with the characteristic of growing in the same direction. Thus sealskins can be attached to the bottom of the skis and the skis will slide in one direction and grip in the reverse direction. Modern skins are manufactured using synthetic materials designed to exhibit the same characteristics and are very efficient. Most modern skins are attached either by hooks or by an adhesive backing. Col-Tex and Ramer are two widely available brands of skins that are popular with ski tourers.

For steep climbs or when walking long distances it is much less tiring on one's legs to have a ski binding that allows the heel of your boot to lift as you slide your feet backwards and forwards. There are some excellent ski touring bindings available, and a visit to any good ski mountaineering shop will allow you to inspect the various models. A few brands that I am familiar with and can recommend are the Tyrolia, Ramer, Petzl, Marker and Izere. With a good ski binding and a good pair of skins you are ready to walk up the slopes.

98a

98b

98c

98a–c: Walking on flat terrain using skins.

1 Walking on flat terrain using skins

Prior to climbing with skins, it is best to learn to walk with them on the flat. Start on level terrain, standing with one foot pushed forward (picture 98a). Plant your ski pole to the side of the foot of your forward ski and lift the heel of your rear foot (left ski, right ski pole and vice-versa). Now lean your body slightly forward and slide your rear ski forward, simultaneously bringing your rear ski pole forward (picture 98b). Transfer your weight on to this foot as you continue to push this foot forward, and allow your rear heel to lift. Now slide your new rear ski forward and repeat the same series of movements (picture 98c), so that you are gliding along, placing one foot before the other.

Note

☐ It may seem awkward at first but with very little practice it will become easy to perform.

2 Walking up slopes using skins

Walking up slopes with skins is essentially the same as walking on the flat with skins. The differences are that your upper body should be leaning slightly up the hill and your legs will have to work harder.

Start on a gentle slope and proceed to walk straight up the fall-line of the hill. Be sure to tilt your upper body slightly forwards the entire time you are climbing (picture sequence 99). Repeat the same weight-shifting and ski-sliding movements that you did while walking with the skins on the flat and walk up the hill, concentrating on finding the natural rhythm of sliding your skis forward.

Special tips

● You may at first find your rear ski sliding backwards when you are ready to bring it forward. It is only a matter of trial and error to find the right position of your upper body to ensure a grip of the skins on the snow as you transfer your weight from ski to ski. As you continue to practise you should find it easier to prevent the skis from slipping away.

99a

99a–c: Walking up slopes using skins.   99b

99c

100b

100a

100a–c: Walking uphill using bindings with convertible bar adaptor for steep climbs.

100c

- With most ski touring bindings you can easily walk up gentle slopes and certain grades of intermediate slopes. Some of the ski binding companies, such as Tyrolia and Ramer, have convertible bindings, using either plugs or bar extensions that permit easy climbing up steeper slopes (picture sequence 100).

- Walking up steep slopes with skins requires some additional practice in order to refine your weight-shifting movement to prevent the skis from slipping backwards.

- Except on gentle slopes, when climbing up a slope with skins it is usual to walk on a diagonal to the fall-line. The angle of the diagonal depends mainly on the steepness of the slope and the type of ski binding you are using. Bindings that have a steep slope climbing attachment will permit you to climb straighter up the slopes, thereby making the climb easier and saving you time.

- When climbing with skins, always carry a knapsack so that you can tuck the skins away when you are ready for your descent.

- Although you can ski tour on any type of ski there are specialized skis that are designed to easily handle the differing types of snow you generally encounter in out-of-bounds ski areas. These skis normally are shorter, wider and lighter than standard skis. Most major ski manufacturers make an out-of-bounds ski. The skis that I have had the most success with in all snow conditions are the Duret 'Raid Extreme' and the Fischer 'Tour Alpin'.

'Off-piste' precautions

Since skins are used primarily to gain access to the 'off-piste', you must be aware of the precautions that should always be taken whenever you ski out-of-bounds:

- Never ski alone.

- Always let others who remain behind know where you are planning to go and when you are expected to return.

- Check with knowledgeable persons such as mountain rangers or the area ski patrol if it is permissible to ski in the area where you wish to go.

- Check with knowledgeable persons if the snow conditions are safe.

- Avoid going out-of-bounds if the weather is bad or unsettled.

- It is best to go out-of-bounds with ski instructors who specialize in this type of skiing and know the area where you are planning on going, or with certified mountain guides.

- If going with friends and without a guide, take a topographical map of the area, a needle and thread to repair your skins should they tear, a compass, an altimeter, emergency food and clothing and a bright reflecting object that can be seen by rescuers should you become lost or injured. In addition take a rope, crampons and ice axes if the area has crevasses. You should also know how to make emergency splints for injuries.

- If there is any chance of avalanches, you should wear an avalanche transponder or transmitter–Arva 4000, Ortovox, Ramer, Pieps, Elp and RUF make good units–and you should ascertain that your unit operates on the same frequency as the units used by the local rescue services. Have an avalanche cord attached, and make sure you are familiar with avalanche slopes, the dangers of avalanches and the procedures for avalanche rescues.

The ultimate skiing experience

If you have successfully practised most of the exercises in Section Two, then you are now undoubtedly an advanced skier. You not only should be able to confidently ski all the runs on the mountains using various advanced skiing manoeuvres, but also most of the 'off-piste' slopes as well on packed snow conditions. You are therefore ready to enter into a new dimension in skiing, and experience what is for many the ultimate skiing pleasure: skiing powder snow, which is explained in Section Three.

Powder Skiing

In an article I wrote for *Skiing* magazine I tried to capture the feeling that I experienced on a steep, newly discovered powder run in Farellones, Chile, as follows:

'Alone–me, my skis, the mountain, and the soft, delicate snow yielding ever so tenderly as my skis pressed from one silent turn to the next. Down, down, down–all I could see was white, fluffy untracked powder; I was lost in total absorption . . . lost in ecstasy, mindless of the danger of falling and never being found, I continued on, shooting plumes of fine, white mist behind me until exhaustion and concern broke into my consciousness. . . .'

Through the years I've read and heard other vain efforts by skiers wanting to share the joys of their powder descents and I'm convinced that although 'powder' seems to make poets out of skiers, their descriptions fall far short of the reality.

Skiing powder snow is a very personal experience, as the skier develops an intimate relationship with the snow and the mountain. It is certainly exciting, exhilarating and pleasurable. I feel that powder skiing is to skiing what ballet is to dance, for it requires an artistry and finesse of movement, coupled with a strength of body and fluidity of motion.

The basic turn for skiing powder snow is the shortswing turn, as described in Section Two (page 88). All that is necessary to use this turn in powder is to modify the body stance and weight distribution and exaggerate the flexion-extension-flexion movements. Once this is learnt, the next step is to experience the feeling of riding on a soft cushion beneath the skis rather than on a solid surface, and overcoming the fear of not being able to see your skis while they are under the snow. (Except for those instances where snow is flying in your face or you are in 'bottomless' powder, you should always be able to see your ski tips.)

To learn how to ski the powder I therefore recommend that you first learn the modified body stance and then practise traversing and turning uphill in deep snow to experience the feeling of riding on a cushiony base.

There are many ways of initiating turns in powder and in this section I describe 11 approaches. Skiers eventually develop their own styles and ski the powder in ways that feel most secure and comfortable to them, often combining various aspects of the different powder turns. A very good powder skier will undoubtedly be proficient in many of these turns and will let the type and depth of snow and steepness of the terrain dictate which turn to utilize.

The turn that can be used in just about every powder snow condition, and therefore is the most versatile turn, emphasizes up-unweighting. I refer to it as the basic down-up-down powder turn. This is the turn that I feel every new powder skier should learn, use and master. Once you can ski powder confidently with the basic down-up-down powder turn, you can practise some of the other ten turns.

The basic down-up-down powder turn

1 The traverse position

Pictures 101a and 101b show the modification of the body stance required to ski powder. Picture 101a shows a normal piste traverse position. Picture 101b shows the powder traverse position. The key to skiing powder is to move your centre of gravity backwards so that it is over your heels rather than over your insteps. The way to accomplish this is to sit slightly lower so that your hips are over your heels, with your upper body upright. When you are in the correct position your toes should be brushing lightly against the upper surface of the inside of the ski boots, rather than pressing down on the footbed. It is also necessary to keep your weight evenly distributed over both feet. (This is so that you do not sink lower into the snow on one foot than the other, which could easily cause you to topple over.)

Special tips

- It is easiest to ski powder with your skis close together. As you get more proficient you can adjust the space between your skis to your own liking.

- Keep your arms held wider apart and slightly higher than for the normal piste skiing, and roll both knees slightly uphill so that your skis are edged.

- A common misconception of many novice powder skiers is in thinking that you should always lean backwards so that your legs are against the backs of the boots in order to lighten the pressure on the ski tips. If you ski like that you will lose control of your skis! To maintain control of your skis in powder, particularly on a steep slope or at speed, it is necessary to keep continuous contact between your shins and the fronts of your ski boots.

(However, you should not press as hard against the fronts as you do on the packed snow or on the ice.) The times when it is advisable to lean back against the backs of the ski boots are when skiing in fairly deep snow on a gentle slope, when skiing up a large dip and when skiing on an intermediate pitch in very wet, heavy snow.

- Notice in pictures 101a and 101b that all parts of the body that are uphill remain slightly in front of their downhill counterparts. During shortswing turns your upper body should, of course, be facing downhill the entire time.

Note

- Although shortswing turns are most popular in powder, one can also make large-radius turns. To do so, you should be standing squarer on your skis, which means that your shoulders and hips should be facing more towards your ski tips, in other words, the uphill parts of your body are more level with the downhill parts, as shown in picture 101c. (Skiing large-radius turns is described on page 177.)

2 Traversing

Find a wide stretch of untracked powder on an intermediate grade slope (you can often find this alongside a packed intermediate ski run). Assume the powder position and traverse across the slope in a shallow track (as in picture 102a). You should choose a traverse just steep enough to maintain some speed. While you are traversing, lower your hips (as in picture 102b) so that you feel your heels being pushed into the snow. (When you do that your ski tips will tilt up.) Bounce up from your heels and fully extend your legs (picture 102c) and then lower your hips again over your heels (picture 102d) using an exaggerated flex motion. Continue across the slope, bouncing up off your heels, and then come to a gradual stop in the same traverse.

Do a kick turn and traverse in the opposite direction repeating the same motions. Continue traversing-stopping-kick turning and traversing in the new direction until you have mastered skiing in the powder.

Normal piste traverse position.   101a

Special tips

- I refer to this as the 'dolphin' motion, as the movement resembles that of a dolphin in water.

- Try not to jump or hop when you push up off your heels. The motion should be strong and fluid, and similar to the exaggerated leg pumping used for skating.

- For this exercise there is no pole planting. Keep your arms held wide apart and high enough so that the tips of your ski poles are just out of the snow.

- Be sure to keep your weight evenly distributed on both heels at all times.

- Keep your knees rolled slightly uphill so that your skis are edged. (Do not permit your skis to sideslide.)

101c

Modified powder traverse position for large-radius turns.

Powder traverse position.   101b

102b

102a

102d

102c

102a–d: Traversing in powder using down-up-down bouncing movements.

3 Uphill turns

A Gradual traverse

On the same slope, choose a slightly steeper traverse track and *with your weight on both feet*, start to traverse holding your uphill ski pole vertical, as shown in picture 103a.

When you decide to turn uphill, flex (lower) your hips with an exaggerated motion, as you did in exercise 2 (picture 103b). As you bounce up, dive up and around your ski pole (picture 103c), as you did when learning on packed slopes (page 70), and your skis will turn uphill. Be sure to keep your knees rolled towards the hill so that your skis are well edged. As the skis start to turn uphill begin lowering your hips over your heels so that your heels are pressing into the snow, and steer your skis with your knees until you come to a gradual stop (picture 103d).

103a

103b

103c

103a–d: Turning uphill in powder.

103d

B Steeper traverse

Choose a traverse track slightly steeper than that of exercise 3A and repeat the same manoeuvre. (Try to prevent the skis from turning as you flex your hips; the uphill turn should be made during the strong extension movement.) Ski to a stop with an exaggerated, slow lowering of your hips, pressing your heels into the snow and steering with your knees.

C Steep traverse

Choose a traverse track just off the fall-line and, repeating the same procedures as above, turn your skis uphill and then ski to a stop.

D Starting on fall-line

Face down the fall-line (as in picture 104a). With your weight on both feet gain some momentum. While gliding, and holding the same ski pole forward as you used for the previous exercises, flex (lower) your hips over your heels, as in picture 104b. Repeat the same procedures as above, turning your skis up the hill with an exaggerated extension movement and then stop (pictures 104c, 104d and 104e), steering with your knees and pressing your heels into the snow.

104a   104b

104c

104d

104a–e: Turning uphill to stop, starting on fall-line.

104e

105a

105b

Special tip

● As in the previous exercise, be sure to roll your knees towards the hill during your extension movement, and keep them rolling towards the hill until you stop.

E   Repeat exercises A–D in the opposite direction

105a–e: Turning downhill in powder from a steep traverse.

105e

105c

105d

Special tips

● Exaggerating the flexion-extension-flexion movements facilitates turning the skis in the deep snow.

● At all times maintain your powder position, with your upper body upright, your knees rolled towards the hill (except when skiing straight down the fall-line), your arms held wide apart and high–your hands should be just below shoulder level–your weight evenly distributed on both feet, and crouching slightly so that your centre of gravity is over your heels. Your head should be naturally centred and you should watch where you are skiing.

● Try to flex in a steady, continuous motion so that you do not jerk downwards. (A sudden jerk downwards will result in down-unweighting which may cause your skis to turn uphill.)

● Do not put any weight on your ski pole as you place it in the snow. The ski pole in powder is used primarily to help time and co-ordinate the turn.

● Perform each flexion and extension movement with long, slow strokes. (Do not try to hurry your turn; rather, allow time for your skis to turn.)

4 Downhill turns

Once you can make turns on both sides starting on the fall-line, it is very easy to turn downhill across the fall-line.

A Steep traverse
With your weight on both feet and your skis close together, start in a steep traverse on an intermediate grade slope (picture 105a).

Start to gain momentum and bring your downhill ski pole vertical. When you are ready to turn, lower your hips with a slow, exaggerated motion, simultaneously planting your ski pole (picture 105b). From this low position extend upwards by pushing off your heels, coming up and around your ski pole (exactly as you did for the uphill turn), and your skis will start to turn across the fall-line (picture 105c).

106a–g: Linking downhill turns in powder (inc. overleaf).

106b

106a

Special tip

- Exaggerate your extension movement and perform it more slowly than you do on a packed slope and do not try to rush your skis across the fall-line.

As your skis cross the fall-line, start to flex your hips over your heels (picture 105d) and steer your skis to a stop by rolling your knees uphill while pressing your heels into the snow (picture 105e), as you did for the uphill turn. Now start in a steep traverse to the opposite direction and repeat the turn across the fall-line.

Special tips

- When you make the extension movement, pull up slightly with your outside arm and shoulder so that you feel a stretching along your outside ribcage (picture 105c). This motion helps bring the skis out of the deep or heavy snow.

- As you extend up and around your ski pole, and as you flex after the turn, be sure to keep your upper body upright. If you bend forward at the waist you will weight the fronts of your skis and will probably fall over the fronts of your skis as the tips catch in the snow.

- At no time during the turn should your skis be absolutely flat on the snow! Start traversing with your knees rolled towards the hill so that your skis are edged. As your skis cross the fall-line during the extension, roll your knees in the direction of the turn and keep them rolling over until they end up pointing uphill so that your skis are well edged as you flex and complete the turn.

- Although the skis are edged, you should not ride on their edges as you do on packed snow. When you press down on your heels, the entire width of the ski bottom should compress the snow beneath it. (The reasons we keep the skis on their edges is to enable the ski to carve a turn, rather than make a skid turn, and to prevent catching the downhill ski edge, which usually leads to an awkward fall.)

B   Moderate traverse

Start on a traverse track less steep than the track chosen for exercise 4A and repeat the turn across the fall-line, stopping at the end of the turn. Repeat on the opposite side.

C   Linking two turns

Once you can make a controlled turn to each side you can link two turns.

Start in the same moderate traverse track chosen for exercise 4B, pick up speed (picture 106a), and make the same turn. Lower your hips and plant your downhill ski pole (picture 106b),

bounce off your heels, come up and around your ski pole (picture 106c) and allow the skis to turn across the fall-line. (At all times you should be facing downhill.) As your skis cross the fall-line, begin lowering your hips (picture 106d) and, rather than steering your skis to a stop as you did in the previous exercise, bring your new downhill ski pole vertical (picture 106e), and push again off your heels, up and around the pole (picture 106f) and make another downhill turn (picture 106g).

At the completion of this turn, continue lowering your hips and steer your skis to a stop.

106d

106c

106e

106f

106g

D Skiing a series of shortswing turns

When you feel confident making two turns, try to make three and then four turns before stopping. The important point to remember is not to *rush* the turns. Making a turn in powder is somewhat analogous to steering a sailboat, in other words, when you push the tiller of the sailboat to one side (or turn the wheel), the boat does not swing about instantly, but rather swings in a slow, smooth arc. Likewise, when making a powder turn, you should initiate the turn with the extension movement, and then allow the skis to turn across the fall-line in a slow, smooth arc.

When you can make four controlled turns without falling, you should choose a long intermediate-grade powder slope and ski it making slow, graceful shortswing turns, using lots of exaggerated down-up-down movements.

E Shortswing turns on advanced intermediate slopes

Skiing in powder is easier on steeper slopes than on moderately pitched slopes. The steepness allows your skis to slide faster which enables you to turn more easily (while the powder provides resistance which prevents you from going too fast). Once you can comfortably ski the powder on an intermediate-grade slope it should be very easy to do so on an advanced-intermediate grade.

Choose an advanced-intermediate grade slope of untracked powder and make three or four turns and then stop. Repeat until you have mastered this; then link a series of shortswing turns down the slope, moderating the amount of down-up-down movements and concentrating on skiing slowly and finishing each turn in complete control.

Note

☐ As mentioned previously, this is the standard powder turn that is useful on practically every type of snow condition. So practise and perfect this manoeuvre on all the powder pistes and safe 'off-pistes' that you can, and enjoy yourself as you frolic with the other 'powder hounds'.

When you feel that you have mastered this turn you can practise the other ways of initiating turns in powder, and subsequently assimilate those movements that you find the easiest into your own personal powder style.

Punching through the powder

Punching through the powder is simply a modification of the basic down-up-down powder turn. To punch your turns you continually face downhill making shortswing turns close to the fall-line while you punch 'uppercuts' with your hands, arms and shoulders. This is usually performed without pole planting.

The punching action helps to pull your skis out of the snow and is often used on intermediate-grade slopes, or less, and in deep or heavy snow. Because the skis stay close to the fall-line, in order to avoid picking up too much speed, one generally does not punch on very steep slopes except in very deep powder.

To ski with punching, start on a steep traverse on an intermediate-grade slope of untracked powder. Pick up speed, lower your hips and, as you start your leg and hip extension, punch your outside hand, arm and shoulder up and slightly towards the downhill turn so that you feel a strong pull on your outside ribcage (as can be seen in pictures 107a and 107b). As your skis approach the fall-line, begin lowering your hips and lowering your arm. When your skis cross the fall-line, extend your legs and hips and punch your new outside hand, arm and shoulder up and slightly towards the downhill turn. Continue these motions down the slope.

In picture sequence 107 I am skiing a few tight shortswing turns, punching uppercuts. Notice how my hands and arms end up above my shoulders and notice also how they co-ordinate with my hip extension to help pull my skis out of the snow.

107a   107b

107c

107d

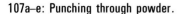
107a–e: Punching through powder.

107e

The jet turn in powder and crust

As I mentioned in discussing the jet turn in Section Two, I usually ski jet turns when skiing through evergreen glades in deep powder. I also ski jet turns in heavy snow, in wet snow and in certain breakable crust conditions.

The jet turn is very effective for these snow conditions because during the turn the tips of the skis are shot out of the snow. In heavy or wet snow this breaks the bond between the skis and the snow and makes it easier to turn the skis around. Furthermore, because your ski tips are shot forward, your weight is much further back on your skis, which prevents the tips from digging into the snow (nose-diving). On breakable crust, the jetting action forces the inside edges of the skis to cut through the surface, reducing the risk of catching the outside edge during the turn, as can be seen in picture 108b. In the evergreen glades, shooting the tips out of the snow helps reduce the danger of hidden branches beneath the snow catching the ski tips.

To learn to make the jet turn you should practise the exercises starting on page 122 of Section Two. Once you can make correct jet turns on the packed slopes, it is simple to use the turn for powder skiing.

Picture sequence 109 shows some jet turns in powder. Notice how the skis shoot forward and turn downhill (pictures 109b and 109d) while the upper body remains quite still. As you are completing the turn it is very important that you recover your correct powder position with your shins touching against the fronts of your ski boots in order to maintain control of your skis (picture 109e).

Naturally, in deep powder, when you plant your ski pole you cannot lean all your weight on it in order to push off to recover your upper body position over your skis at the end of the turn, because when you lean on the ski pole it will sink into the snow. Nonetheless, when performing a jet turn in powder you do plant the ski pole and use the pole plant more as a timing manoeuvre (picture 109a).

Special tip

- If the snow is compressible, as it will be in most snow conditions other than very fine, light, dry, winter powder, your ski pole baskets will have some resistance as they sink in the snow, which can help you push off to recover your body position. Your recovery must be accomplished by contracting your stomach muscles in the same way that you use your stomach muscles when performing situps. (It is therefore a good idea to tone up your stomach muscles.)

Jet turn practice

On an intermediate-grade slope of untracked powder, practise making one jet turn across the fall-line and ski to a stop. Repeat on the other side and then link two jet turns. When you feel that you can perform the manoeuvre in control, link a series of jet turns down the slope and then ski them as often as possible until you master the manoeuvre.

Special tip

- As you jet your skis out, steer the skis into the turn with your feet and roll your knees across the fall-line so that your skis are well edged throughout the turn. Try to use the entire bottom of the skis to carve through, and press against the snow during the turn.

Notes

- One of my more enjoyable delights when skiing deep powder is to jet turn at speed off the crests of small rolling hills or large mounds and land on the down-slope or in the trough behind the hills. Usually the snow in the trough or on the back of the hill is quite deep, as this is where blown snow collects, and so when you jet turn off the crest and land in this deep snow you normally sink quite some way,

108a

108b

the impact often creating an explosion of swirling snow which can be completely enveloping and momentarily blinding. Should you be accompanied by a friend with a camera, this effect makes a great picture.

☐ When skiing powder in the back-bowls, you will often encounter different types of snow conditions as you ski from one pitch or exposure to another. If the wind has blown up you may, for example, hit some hard-packed snow as you come off a steep slope on to a relatively flat pitch which, because you are sitting down in the 'powder position', can cause your skis to shoot forward. Making a couple of quick jet turns will enable you to recover your control and carry on skiing.

108c

108d

108a–d: Jet turns in breakable crust.

109a

109b

109d

109c

109a–e: Jet turns in powder (see previous page).   109e

Anticipation and banking

When you are facing down the hill making shortswing turns you are automatically skiing with anticipation. If you bank your turns by planting your ski pole further to your side so that you are leaning in towards the centre of the turn, you will find it easier to initiate powder turns.

To learn anticipation and banking, you should practise the exercises described in Section Two (pages 99 and 101). Once you can ski with anticipation and banking on a packed slope, it is easy to use these manoeuvres in the powder.

Anticipation

As noted above, if you ski shortswing turns and are always facing down the fall-line, you are skiing with anticipation. If you are making large-radius turns or if you are starting a turn from a shallow traverse, to anticipate your turn, you must turn your upper body in the direction of the turn as you lower your hips and plant your ski pole. Picture sequence 110 demonstrates the use of anticipation to initiate a turn in untracked powder. Notice in picture 110b how the upper body faces in the direction of the turn during the flexion movement, prior to the extension and before the skis cross the fall-line.

Special tips

● Anticipation makes it easier to initiate a turn – especially useful when skiing in powder.

● If you are skiing large-radius turns with anticipation, you should 'square' your hips and shoulders over your skis as the skis cross the fall-line (see picture 101c).

110b

110a

110a–d: Powder turn using anticipation.
110c
110d

Banking

I love banking turns–both on the piste and in the powder. The reason is that banking lets nature's forces help us initiate the turn, thereby saving lots of self-generated energy.

To bank a turn in the powder you simply hold your arms very wide and plant your downhill pole far to your side, an action requiring your upper body to lean to the inside of the turn as you perform your flexion movement at the start of the turn. By leaning your upper body to your side you are off-setting your weight and centre of gravity in the direction of the turn, thereby making it easier to start your skis turning.

To practise banking your turns in the powder, start on a traverse track and, as you start your flexion movement, reach far to your side as you plant your ski pole so that you must lean your upper body down the hill. Now spring up with the same movements that you use for the basic down-up-down turn and, as your skis turn across the fall-line, roll your knees across the fall-line and bring your upper body over the skis so that you are in a good powder position at the end of the turn and ski to a stop. Repeat this turn in the opposite direction and when you can make the turn equally well to both sides, ski a series of banked turns down the slope.

Special tip

● You can bank your turns skiing either shortswing turns or large-radius turns.

Picture sequence 111 shows banking during a large-radius turn. Notice in pictures 111a–111d how the body leans in towards the centre of the turn as the skis cross the fall-line. Picture sequence 112 shows banking during a shortswing turn on windblown crust.

111a

111a–e: Banking during a large-radius turn in powder.

111b

112a

112b

111c

112c

111d

111e

112d

112a–d: Banking during shortswing turn on windblown crust.

Note

☐ Although I'd known about banked turns for a long time, I learnt to appreciate their value by watching Jean-Claude Killy 'free-skiing' the moguls. I decided that if he chose to ski using banked turns, there must be something to it and so I practised what he was doing and discovered much to my delight a very efficient means of getting into a turn, equally good on moguls, powder, and 'off-piste' snow.

Powder wedeln

Wedelning on a *packed* slope is performed with the skis kept almost flat to the surface, with very little down-up-down movements and with quick motions of the skis, all of which are contrary to what should normally be done in powder. However, there are times when fine, light powder falls on a solid base surface and if a skier is descending an intermediate-grade slope it is possible to keep the skis in the snow, riding on the hidden surface, and to 'powder wedeln' down the fall-line.

To wedeln in powder you should ski the basic shortswing motion, facing constantly down the fall-line and using only a very small amount of down-up movement. Swing your skis on wider arcs than you would swing on the packed snow, and roll your skis from one set of edges to the other (by steering with your knees and feet) in order not to catch the outside ski edges in the resisting snow.

Picture sequence 113 shows a series of powder wedeln turns. Notice how the skis remain in the snow and how little the body moves as the skis swing from one turn to the next.

113a   113b

113c

113a–d: Series of powder wedeln turns.   113d

Special tips

● To wedeln in the powder, you should be in the 'powder position' and therefore should sit slightly lower than you do when piste wedelning in order that your centre of gravity is over your heels rather than over the middle of your feet.

● Keep your feet close together and plant your ski poles at your side, holding your arms wide.

● If you feel that you are going too fast or are starting to lose control, exaggerate your down-up-down movements and swing a few large turns to get back in control, and then either stop or carry on down the slope using either the powder wedeln or the basic down-up-down turn.

Note

☐ When I'm skiing in evergreen glades I often powder wedeln to make some quick turns to get around closely spaced trees. In fact, I prefer to powder wedeln at every opportunity I can, as this is one of the most efficient means of turning one's skis using the least amount of energy.

Modified avalement

To learn to make avalement turns practise the exercises starting on page 110 of Section Two. Once you can ski using avalement you will find it useful for skiing powder, particularly powder that has recently fallen on a mogul field or on a run that contains rocks, tree stumps or logs. When snow falls it covers everything on the slope with what appears to be a uniformly thick white carpet. Of course this is deceptive. Beneath this white carpet lie many undulations and obstacles.

Avalement is the answer to these troublesome objects; for once you have accustomed your feet, knees and hips to 'avaler' these unseen bumps, you can ski the runs with carefree abandon, swallowing (or absorbing) every uneven surface that you encounter, making avalement turns off the tops of each object hidden beneath the snow.

It is also possible to use an avalement movement as a means of making very smooth, controlled turns, in deep obstacle-free powder. Picture sequence 114 demonstrates a series of modified avalement turns in powder.

Since there are no moguls in the powder to compress your knees, the standard avalement motion must be modified. To learn to ski modified avalement in the powder start on an intermediate-grade slope of at least boot-top deep untracked powder with your weight on both feet. In order to ski this modified avalement, you must alter your basic powder stance by sitting back just a little further and bending your torso slightly forward from your waist so that your weight is still over your heels. Start to traverse and gather speed. When you are ready to turn, rather than lowering your hips (as you do for the basic down-up-down powder turn), pull your knees up towards your chest and plant your downhill ski pole at the same time (as in picture 114b). When your knees are drawn up, roll them across the fall-line (picture 114c) and push your legs down again in the new traverse direction exactly as you do at the end of the standard avalement turn, and continue to press down while your skis are turning (picture 114d). As you complete the turn across the fall-line, again plant your downhill ski pole and draw your knees towards your chest (picture 114e), roll them across the fall-line and press your legs down, turning in the new direction (picture 114f).

Continue these modified avalement turns down the slope.

Special tips

● It is best to ski this technique close to the fall-line, keeping your upper body facing down the fall-line.

● Try to develop a smooth, continuous rhythm as you go from one turn to the next.

● Notice that the turn is essentially the same as the standard avalement turn, except that the stomach and thigh muscles are used to pull the knees towards the chest rather than using a mogul to push the knees towards the chest. It therefore helps to train in the off-season to develop strong, toned stomach and thigh muscles.

● The reason one bends slightly forwards from the waist is to prevent the weight from shifting too far backwards—with a subsequent loss of ski control—when the legs are compressed upwards.

Notes

☐ I only discovered this technique a few years ago while skiing the out-of-bounds with an Austrian friend. His style intrigued me as he skied very differently from the way I did and he was very competent in the deep snow conditions that we encountered. In analysing how he turned, I realized that he was actually skiing a modified avalement in the powder. Since then I have noticed other skiers skiing this way and have discovered that this is one of the techniques taught in Austria to ski in deep and heavy powder. I especially like to ski modified avalement when skiing on moderate slopes in knee- and thigh-deep snow and in thin wind- or sun-affected crust conditions.

☐ As visibility is often very poor when it is
snowing, learning to ski by feel rather than by
sight will enable you to ski safely during
snowstorms or whiteout conditions, with the
further benefit of permitting you to cut first
tracks in the newly fallen powder while the
other skiers await the sunshine.

114b

114a

114c

114d

114a–f: Modified avalement turns in powder.   114e

114f

The jump turn

Perhaps the most natural way to turn your skis is to jump them out of the snow, turn them in the air and land in the new direction. As I have mentioned in Sections One and Two, this is the way I was taught to ski and I have been forever grateful to my early instructors, as not only did I instantly learn to turn my skis parallel, but I have also used this turn ever since for getting through difficult snow conditions.

The problem with always skiing jump turns is that it is both very tiring, since you are jumping against the pull of gravity, and hard on the knees, since they must absorb and cushion the landings. Also, modern skis are designed to turn so easily that in most snow conditions it is unnecessary to jump around to get your skis from one traverse to the next. There are, however, snow conditions in which it is very difficult to turn easily using any of the previously explained techniques. In such conditions the jump turn can always be employed and therefore every advanced skier who plans to ski 'off-piste' snow and steep gullies should be thoroughly familiar and comfortable with the jump turn.

Conditions that can require the jump turn to be used are as follows: **1**–very heavy snow (either moist or wind-packed) on a moderate to steep incline: the jump turn is used to get the skis out of the heavy snow so as to turn them easily in the air; **2**–hard surfaces of wind-packed snow with lots of wind-ridges: the jump turn is used to jump over the ridges and turn in the air; **3**–on non-supporting breakable crust over a powder base: this is the trickiest because it requires great strength (to break up through the crust) and precise edge control when landing (so as to not catch the outside ski edge); **4**–in steep, narrow gullies: to turn the skis in a tight radius without gaining momentum; **5**–in steep gullies or mountain faces with difficult conditions (such as crust, heavy powder, protruding rocks, large frozen snow granules, and wind-ridges) and in spring conditions when the sun has left only a narrow strip of snow remaining (as in picture sequence 117).

To learn to jump turn, practise on an advanced-intermediate packed slope and then practise on a difficult packed slope. To perform the jump turn, execute the down-up-down turn using an explosive up-motion so that the skis lift off the snow.

On an advanced-intermediate slope, begin traversing, and start to lower your hips, simultaneously planting your downhill ski pole at your side (as shown in picture 115a). Now jump up and around your ski pole (picture 115b), lifting your skis off the snow and turning your skis while they are in the air (picture 115c). Land in the new traverse position with your knees rolled uphill and your hips and knees cushioning the impact of the landing (pictures 115d and 115e). Now repeat this jump turn in the opposite direction.

When practising on the difficult (black coded) slopes face your upper body down the fall-line and plant your ski pole further back than you did on the advanced-intermediate grade slope so as to use anticipation to help you jump in a tighter radius.

115a

115a–e (inc. overleaf): Jump turn on packed slope. 115b

115c

115d

116b

116a–d: Jump turn on thin crust snow conditions.

116a

115e

116c

116d

Notes

☐ Once you can jump turn on the packed slopes, practise jump turning in light powder snow and then practise in heavy snow.

☐ Practise on short stretches of breakable crust close to the packed slopes in order to acquire the finesse required to ski in these conditions before venturing off into the back-bowls.

☐ After the wind has blown up, or in the springtime when the hot, blazing sun has altered the texture of the exposed powder faces, to get to a good 'off-piste' powder slope, it is sometimes necessary to ski through some stretches of very tricky snow. Knowing how to jump turn can therefore be extremely useful, permitting you to venture on undaunted while other skiers turn back.

117a

117b

117a–c: Jump turn on narrow strip of snow on steep gully. 117c

The power turn
(knee steering)

Once you have skied long enough to have developed refined body movement, balance and edge control, and are competent at higher speeds, it is possible to ski in various powder conditions merely by steering your knees using no noticeable up movements or down movements. This technique, which I call the power turn or knee steering, is a very tireless way of skiing, especially when performed in light or medium-light powder. Because the power turn does not cause the skis to turn rapidly across the fall-line, this turn does not slow the skier down as much as most of the other turns do, and hence is best skied on intermediate-grade slopes in powder which is at least knee deep or on steep slopes in thigh- or waist-deep powder, as the resistance of the snow against the body is used to prevent the skier from going too fast.

Notes

☐ This is the turn I almost always employ when skiing short, very steep gullies in hip- or waist-deep snow.

☐ The power turn makes use of momentum and the pull of gravity to help get the skis through the turns, and hence is most often used when skiing quickly or dynamically.

Power turn practice

Practise on an easy intermediate slope on packed snow. Start by traversing in a good piste position with your weight evenly distributed on both feet, as shown in picture 118a. When you are ready to turn, press both knees down the fall-line (picture 118b) and continue to roll your knees across the fall-line as the skis turn (picture 118c). At all times press down on your insteps so that your skis are in good contact with the snow. Continue to steer your skis with your knees (picture 118d) as you turn your skis uphill, and when you are ready for the next turn again press both knees down the fall-line and steer your skis with your knees through the next turn.

118a

118b

Special tips

● If you wish to make large-radius turns, keep your upper body 'square' to your skis (hips and shoulders facing towards your ski shovels).

● If you wish to make short-radius turns, keep your upper body facing down the fall-line.

Once you can perform this turn on the packed slopes, assume the powder position on your skis and practise on an easy intermediate-grade slope in boot-top-deep powder. When you can make power turns in good control on these slopes, you can practise on steeper slopes in deeper powder, skiing close to the fall-line.

118a–d: Power turns (knee steering) on packed slope.

118d

Down-unweighting

German, Austrian and some American ski schools for years taught down-unweighting as the basic means of unweighting the skis when turning across the fall-line. Down-unweighting, which I have also heard referred to as the magic turn, works, and though I don't feel it should be the basic means of initiating turns, I do feel it is valuable for advanced skiers to know. Aside from being a very smooth way to turn in certain powder conditions, down-unweighting helps to teach skiers to press the skis into the snow, which is very necessary for maintaining control after a turn, regardless of which method is used for initiating the turn.

Down-unweighting results when one very rapidly sinks down. The effect of the quick down movement momentarily unweights the skis (a standard visual demonstration is to stand on a pair of scales and rapidly lower your hips and watch the weight indicator drop). By making use of this phenomenon for skiing, at the same time as you rapidly lower your hips, you can steer your skis across the fall-line.

Down-unweighting is an alternative technique for skiing moguls (as you can down-unweight and turn around the moguls) and is the quickest way to make a stop turn (which can be very useful to advanced skiers skiing in areas with cliffs and drop-offs). It also is an alternative way of smoothly skiing an intermediate-grade powder slope.

119a

119b

1 The stop turn using down-unweighting

Start off facing down the fall-line and begin to gather speed (picture 119a). At the point you wish to stop, rapidly sink your hips down and twist your feet across the fall-line (picture 119b). Continue rolling your knees so that your skis are well edged, and keep your upper body facing and leaning down the fall-line (picture 119c). Try to come to a stop as quickly as possible.

Repeat this manoeuvre, stopping on the opposite side.

119a–c: Stop turn using down-unweighting.   119c

120a

120b

2   Turning across the fall-line

It is best to learn to make down-unweighted turns on a packed slope and, when you can control your turn and speed, to practise on an intermediate-grade powder slope.

On a packed intermediate-grade slope, start to traverse (picture 120a). When you are ready to turn, plant your downhill ski pole and *rapidly* lower your hips (picture 120b). At the same time, roll your knees across the fall-line and press your skis down into the snow. As your skis cross the fall-line start to raise your hips to a neutral position (picture 120c) and finish the turn in a good traverse position, ready for the next turn (picture 120d).

Make a series of turns on the packed slope and then, if you wish, practise on some small mogul fields, turning around the moguls.

When you feel you can make good down-unweighted turns, seek out an intermediate-grade powder slope and practise making smooth, round turns, down-unweighting at the start of each turn and returning to a neutral position as the skis cross the fall-line.

Once you feel comfortable down-unweighting, you will have an additional means of turning in powder. Picture sequence 121 shows a set of linked down-unweighted turns in powder.

120c

120d

120a–d: Turning across fall-line using down-unweighting (on packed slope).

Note

☐ Apart from the quick down-unweighted stop turn, smooth down-unweighting generally produces long, round turns and therefore you tend to pick up speed during this manoeuvre. Consequently, you should perform these turns on slopes that are not too steep.

121d

121a

121b

121e

121c

121a–f: Down-unweighted turns in powder (see previous page).

121f

Large-radius turns

What with the fashionable trends in ski equipment and techniques being followed by so many, it is a joy for me to see some old-time skier skiing the 'off-piste' powder slopes in baggy trousers, a baggy sweater with a nylon shirt tied around their waist, leather ski boots and long poles with big baskets, executing very large, neatly rounded turns, in perfect control and obviously having at least as much pleasure as we 'modernists'.

True, you cannot ski narrow gullies making large-radius turns, nor very steep slopes (as you will pick up too much speed), but who cares! Certainly not the large-radius type skier, who is gracefully and joyfully carving his sprawling signature on the rolling hills and moderate-pitched slopes that account for most of the 'off-piste' terrain.

Large-radius turns can, of course, also be made with modern equipment. What is required is patience during the turn.

For the position on the skis required to make large-radius turns, refer to picture 101c on page 150 of Section Three. Note that the shoulders and hips face towards the shovels of the skis more than they do for the shortswing position. This is referred to as being 'square' to the skis.

To learn to make large-radius turns, practise on an easy intermediate slope. Start traversing with your arms held comfortably in the 'tray holding' position and your body quite square to your skis (picture 122a). When you are ready to turn, flex your knees and plant your ski pole at your side and not too far away from the skis (picture 122b) and extend up, forwards and slightly around the planted ski pole (picture 122c). As your skis are turning, keep your hips and shoulders facing your ski tips and allow the skis to swing a large, graceful arc, steering gently with your knees and feet (picture 122d). As you complete the turn continue traversing (picture 122e), and then repeat the same motion in the opposite direction, keeping your hips and shoulders quite square to your skis. Continue linking the large turns down the slope.

Once you can perform this manoeuvre on the packed slope, it is very easy to make large-radius turns in the powder. So seek out an intermediate-grade powder slope and make a series of graceful, linked large-radius turns as you negotiate the untraced powder. Picture sequence 123 shows a large-radius turn in powder snow.

Note

☐ Many large-radius turn skiers are also keen on ski trekking the out-of-bounds (*ski randonée*) and, after climbing up some distant peak, have acres of space to swing lazily down the virgin powder slopes making as wide a track as they care to without upsetting the lift-serviced shortswing skiers, who get terribly irritated if someone cuts their personalized curlicues.

122a

122b

122a–e (inc. overleaf): Large-radius turns on packed slope.

122c

122d

122e

123a

123b

123c

123d

123f

123e

123a–f: Large-radius powder turns (page 177).

Breakable crust turns
(Skiing on the uphill edge of uphill ski)

Skiing breakable crust is an art, and, like any art, requires lots of practice in addition to basic talent, to achieve a high level of accomplishment. I have already described a number of different ways of skiing breakable crust, namely, the stem turn, the jet turn, and the jump turn. Another way to ski the breakable crust is to make the turns on the inside edge of the inside ski so that you are always skiing on the uphill edge of the uphill ski. (For an understanding of inside/outside ski, refer to fig 6 and picture sequence 37, pages 62–3.)

The advantage of skiing in this manner is that you can maintain a constant rhythm and make smooth turns while limiting the risk of catching the outside edge in the crust. Because this manoeuvre is almost acrobatic–since it requires very good balance and precise edge control–it is best to first learn the other above-mentioned techniques of initiating turns on this type of snow surface. When you have had enough experience skiing breakable crust, so that it is no longer menacing, you should practise turning on the uphill edge of the uphill ski on a packed slope. Refer back to page 129 of Section Two and

practise exercises 1A, 1B, 1C, 2A and 3A.

Once you have mastered these exercises and can ski and turn on the uphill edge of the uphill ski on the packed slopes, you can practise on the packed slopes making parallel turns on this uphill edge with your skis held together.

1 Downhill turns on the inside edge of the inside ski

A Turns on packed slopes
Start on an intermediate slope in a traverse position with your weight on the uphill edge of the uphill ski.

Special tip

● On the packed slopes your weight should be over the middle of your uphill foot. When you perform this on the crust you should have your weight slightly further backwards.

Start to traverse and when you are ready to turn, lower your hips and plant your downhill ski pole at your side (picture 124a). Extend up and around your ski pole, bank your turn by leaning to the inside of the turn (picture 124b) and roll your knees across the fall-line. Land on your new

124a–d: Turning on inside edge of inside ski.   124a

124b

uphill edge (picture 124c), flexing your knees and keeping your skis well edged towards the mountain, and ski to a stop (picture 124d).

Repeat this manoeuvre on the opposite side and when it feels comfortable doing this to both sides, link a series of turns down the fall-line, skiing from the uphill edge of one ski to the uphill edge of the other ski as you go from one traverse to the next.

B Turns in powder

When you can perform this manoeuvre on a packed slope, practise the same exercises on an intermediate-grade slope of ankle-deep powder.

Special tip

● Assume the powder position, so that your weight is over your heels.

C Turns on breakable crust

When you can perform this manoeuvre in the powder, seek out a gentle slope of breakable crust and practise the same exercises as above. Position your body so that your weight has moved back towards your heels in order to keep your ski tips lightly weighted.

When you can safely and confidently ski down this slope, seek out an intermediate-grade slope of breakable crust and perform the same exercises as above. Once you can link a series of smooth turns, skiing in complete control, you can venture off into the out-of-bounds areas knowing that you are capable of skiing any condition you may encounter.

Picture sequence 125 demonstrates a series of linked inside edge turns on an intermediate-grade slope of crusted powder. Notice how the weight is balanced over the heel of the uphill foot. Picture sequence 126 demonstrates how this turn can be used to ski tricky windblown, breakable crust confidently.

124c

124d

125a

125b

125c

125d

126a

126b

125a–e: Skiing inside edge turns on crusted powder (see page 181). 125e

126c

126d

126a–d: Skiing inside edge turns on windblown crust (see page 181).

127a

127b

127c

127d

127e

127f

127g

127h

127i

127a–i: Combined advanced-skiing manoeuvres on steep, wind-ridged glacier.

Special tips

- This manoeuvre is generally skied fairly dynamically, using shortswing turns, so that the end of one turn is the start of the next turn. Because the breakable crust is so inconsistent it is best to push off the edge as soon as possible after crossing the fall-line, riding the edge only as long as is necessary to complete the turn.

- Try to keep your knees well inclined towards the mountain at the start and end of the turn so that your skis are extensively edged in order not to catch the outside edge.

- Your ski boots should fit as snugly as possible so that you have instant response between your feet and your skis.

- As this is a fast, delicate manoeuvre it is best to use it when skiing gentle or medium-grade slopes, using the jet turn or jump turn on steep slopes.

- You can combine this manoeuvre with the other advanced-skiing manoeuvres to ski difficult 'off-piste' slopes, as in picture sequence 127.

The final word

In the Introduction, I stated that the ultimate goal of this book is to help you reach a level of competence which enables you to safely ski every type of snow and slope that you may encounter.

I have therefore tried to include as much of the information and as many of the hints that I've learnt and accumulated through the years as possible, and to pass these on to you in as clear a way as I am capable.

In Section Two, I've described all those advanced skiing manoeuvres which I feel are useful to help you become more proficient as a skier. I do not profess to have explained every last way of initiating a turn, as there are many personalized styles of skiing.

In describing the powder turns, I haven't discussed a turn once taught in Japan as the dolphin turn, nor the turn that I refer to as the water skiing technique, whereby one sits well back against the back of the boots and flicks the ski tips across the fall-line. Instead in Section Three I limited myself to describing the 11 turns that I feel are the most useful to aspiring powder and 'off-piste' skiers. With these turns you should be able to have fun, and safely ski anywhere your fancy takes you.

Whereas a poet would be able to capture in descriptive and evocative phrases the joys of skiing the 'off-piste', far from the lifts and skier-packed ski slopes, and thus share these joys with you, I have tried, via the many ski exercises, photographs and explanations, to make it easy for you to acquire the necessary skills so that you can experience these joys yourself.

Index

Page numbers in italic type refer to illustrations